Online Marketing Techniques for Real Estate Agents & Brokers

Insider Secrets You Need to Know to Take Your Business to the Next Level

By Karen F. Vieira, PhD

Online Marketing Techniques for Real Estate Agents & Brokers: Insider Secrets You Need to Know to Take Your Business to the Next Level

ISBN-13: 978-1-60138-126-2   ISBN-10: 1-60138-126-3

Library of Congress Cataloging-in-Publication Data

Vieira, Karen F. (Karen Frances), 1978-
  Online marketing techniques for real estate agents and brokers: insider secrets you need to know to take your business to the next level / by Karen F. Vieira.
      p. cm.
Includes bibliographical references and index.
ISBN-13: 978-1-60138-126-2 (alk. paper)
ISBN-10: 1-60138-126-3 (alk. paper)
1. Real estate business--Marketing. 2. Internet marketing. I. Title.

HD1375.V54 2008
333.33068'8--dc22
                              2008009367

Printed in the United States

Table of Contents

Foreword 6

Introduction... 11

CHAPTER 1:
Why Market Online? 17

CHAPTER 2:
Creating Your Branding 31

CHAPTER 3:
Your Public Profiffiile 47

CHAPTER 4:
ONLINE DIRECTORIES 59

CHAPTER 5:
UNDERSTANDING SEARCH ENGINES 69

CHAPTER 6:
SEARCH ENGINE OPTIMIZATION 93

CHAPTER 7:
BUILDING A NEW WEB SITE 117

CHAPTER 8:
GENERATING WEB SITE TRAFFIFIFIFFIIC 125

CHAPTER 9:
EFFECTIVELY USING YOUR LIST 149

CHAPTER 10:
PAY-PER-CLICK MARKETING 163

CHAPTER 11:
Banner Advertising 175

CHAPTER 12:
Affiffliliate Programs 201

CHAPTER 13:
Blogging 217

CHAPTER 14:
Unlocking the Secrets of eBay 235

CHAPTER 15:
Hiring Help for Less 243

Conclusion 257

Bibliography 275

Biography 281

Index 283

FOREWORD

Jim Kimmons

Most real estate agents and brokers are struggling to adapt to the new world of Internet marketing. The old "tried and true" media and methods seem to be losing ground, while terms like "Pay-Per-Click" and "Search Engine Optimization" clamor for our attention.

The term "information overload" takes on a whole new meaning when a Realtor begins to research online marketing, Web sites, and blogs. Because of the huge volume of new material and the fast evolution of technology, it is a very disconcerting proposition. What do you need to do, how is it done, and how much time, effort, and money will be expended?

Dr. Karen Vieira, in *Online Marketing for Real Estate Agents & Brokers*, provides aid and just the right amount of information. The book is fast-paced, with an overview of everything from basic HTML tips through blogging for market development. The information is enough to get you into the process, guide you along the way, and provide you with the necessary resources to get it done. It's an organized plan and instruction manual to get you going without information overload.

Beginning with an introduction to the Internet and the methods of marketing online, Vieira provides precisely the information you need to make the decision to take the plunge. Once you know what you want to do, specific guidance is provided on how to do it. She offers unbiased advice with decisions about what you can do yourself and when you may want to hire professional help. Resources are supplied for locating, interviewing, and selecting Web designers, search engine experts, and Internet marketing professionals.

The advice included in the book concerning SEO, or Search Engine Optimization, is right on track. As a consultant to Realtors in Web marketing, SEO, and Pay-Per-Click (PPC), I have been exposed to just about every scam out there. This book will help you to avoid them. Without boring you to death, the mechanics of how search engines work are explained. Knowing what these tools are doing behind the scenes greatly increases your chances of successful positioning your business at the top of search results for your real estate related, and very competitive, search terms.

There are some very simple, yet critical, rules and techniques that can help your site or blog to achieve free search engine exposure. These techniques are outlined for you in this book, and when you make them a part of your early planning and Web site design process, you will get the results you want. I know that the suggestions included in this book work because they are the tools I use on my own personal real estate site. There is no Black Hat, no scamming the search engines, just rock-solid design and writing tools that will work.

The advantage point to using the Web in your marketing plan is that your site can present a larger-than-life presence. The Internet is a great equalizing force for marketers. You can, through the utilization of the techniques and tools in this book, end up at the top of search engine results for "YourTown real estate." You can build an online presence at little or no cost that rivals the largest brokerage in the area. If the design and content are right, then it is just about getting the visitors to the site. You'll learn about PPC marketing and why it is highly effective at bringing a real estate buyer or seller to your site precisely when they are ready to act. This gets you going while your SEO tactics are taking hold. It is a plan and a process, and with *Online Marketing for Real Estate Agents & Brokers*, you will get the information you need to make it work.

The chapter on blogging alone is worth the cost of the book. Read it carefully and think about the promises that blogging holds for the real estate professional. There isn't a better way to position yourself as a professional and your community's real estate expert. You will get guidance on how to set up your blog, what kind of content should be included, and how to get it up and running free and fast.

Once you have put together your marketing plan and begin to have a presence online, you may want to enhance your marketing with banner ads on other sites or do cooperative banner advertising with other local, non-competing businesses. Everything you need to know about online marketing is included in this book. There is even instruction for implementing ads on your site that will generate revenue to help offset your costs of maintaining your Web presence.

The real estate professional of the future will not be able to rely on handing out business cards, joining clubs, and shaking hands. When more than 80 percent of your potential clients are using the Internet to gather real estate information, can you afford to be absent?

Jim Kimmons
Real Estate Broker
www.RealEstateBusinessSuccess.com
http://realestate.About.com
jimkimmons@gmail.com
866-503-2260

Jim Kimmons is a working real estate broker in Taos, New Mexico and the Real Estate Business Guide writer for the New York Times Web site (**http://realestate.About.com**). He consults with real estate professionals in making the transition to the effective use of all types of technology in real estate. You can visit his consulting Web site at: **www. RealEstateBusinessSuccess.com**.

Introduction

Marketing your real estate services and listings online can make a dramatic difference in your income. The Internet is a great marketing tool for most consumer products or services, but like any tool, it will take time to learn how to use it. You do not have to be an expert to be successful. The Internet has the ability to make or break you based on how you go about using it as a resource. The ability to locate interested consumers and direct them to your Web site is a priceless advantage, and if you are not yet utilizing Internet marketing, you are missing out. The way real estate is marketed, bought, and sold is being revolutionized by the Internet, and the way real estate agents do business is being changed forever.

The Internet is just one tool — albeit a vital tool — in real estate marketing that all real estate agents and brokers must analyze to decide whether marketing their listings and services online offers a great enough return on the investment in marketing costs. Many real estate agents and brokers who market heavily online and have a strong Internet presence in their local area have seen a corresponding increase in their sales and their income, as well as a decrease in expenditures on items such as newspaper advertisements and gas used on wasted trips. Often, real estate service providers are concerned that promoting their Web sites will cost them a fortune that they will not be able to recover in corresponding sales. The truth is quite the opposite: Online marketing of real estate Web sites is a cost-effective way of reaching out to anyone in the world interested in buying or selling property in your local area. An even better feature is that you can manage your online marketing campaign from anywhere in the world.

In today's competitive environment, it is essential to utilize Internet marketing, a presence on the Web, e-mail advertising, and other forms of e-commerce. The Internet is a valuable tool whether you have a brick-and-mortar business or an online business, and a Web site for your business is virtually indispensable in our time of advanced technology. The Internet allows you to promote, advertise, and market your business in a cost-efficient manner, giving you the opportunity to focus your costs on other areas of your business. There is no better marketing tool to place at your disposal. Using the Internet has become more convenient and available. Laptops, cell phones, and even iPods have the ability to connect to the Internet in most public places via a wireless connection. The Internet consists of billions of people who have the ability to reach out directly to your business or organization from anywhere in the world. You have the capability of advertising to all these potential clients for little capital investment.

Having a Web page is not enough as a marketing and advertising strategy. A common misconception among new business owners (or established business owners who are simply not getting the marketing they desire) is the idea that creating a Web site will be enough to promote their company on a mass level. Your Web site is just one small part of your entire marketing plan, depending on your business goals. Many successful real estate agents want to advertise and promote their business on the Web, and for them creating a Web site is good, but if it is not promoted and advertised, no one will ever know about it. By passing out business cards with their Web site URL embossed on them, they are using a traditional marketing campaign to promote their Web site. If they offer a downloadable and printable informational article about their local market from their Web site, or create a place for home buyers to enter information about the home they are looking for so they can be e-mailed each time a home meeting their criteria is listed for sale, they are successfully using their Web site as part of their marketing strategy to meet the goal of increased business.

No one has to be a computer geek, Webmaster, or even have a lot of online experience to quickly learn how to effectively market a business online with a small budget. The best news for real estate agents and brokers is that most potential buyers or sellers of real estate are already searching online. So take advantage of that by providing them with the information and services they are searching for. This book is simple and is designed for individual real estate agents or brokers who do not have an information technology department and are marketing within a limited budget.

This book will show you how to tailor your marketing to not only the World Wide Web, but also to the community you serve. It will help you decide if you want to continue only with your current Web site, or if you need multiple Web sites to accomplish your marketing and financial goals. This book also shows you how to build better Web sites that efficiently market your services. We will cover building new Web sites, a separate blog Web site, using a professional designer, design mistakes to avoid, and how to make your Web site valid using Web standards. You will be instructed on how to build a marketing list, how to capture contact information, how to use an auto-responder, as well as legal considerations for commercial Internet marketing and tips for newsletter and e-zine creation. We will address polling your prospects, selling your prospects on other services, asking for referrals, and keeping your prospects up to date. This book will also cover pay-per-click marketing, how pay-per-click works, why pay-per-click is successful, how to buy advertising, Google™ and Yahoo!® search marketing, Yahoo!® advertising, secret tricks of pay-per-click marketing experts, and cheap pay-per-click marketing tactics.

In Chapter 2, we will discuss branding, some additional Internet marketing techniques, continuity in all your marketing, finding easy-to-remember domain names, and developing a professional image. Chapter 3 will deal with developing your public profile, improving your visibility using online social networking, remaining up to date on trends, current market information, posting on blogs and forums, and utilizing print media in conjunction with the Internet to gain maximum exposure. Chapter 4 will present ideas for keeping your Web sites up to date, getting listed in online phone books, and listing your Web site in major directories. In Chapters 5 and 6, we will delve into understanding search engines, search engine optimization, and how to use search engines to your advantage. Chapters 7 and 8 will instruct the reader on building a new Web site and maximizing traffic to your Web site. Chapter 9 will help you turn Web site traffic into prospects and give you other helpful tips for communicating with your prospects. In Chapter 10, we will get into the world of pay-per-click marketing and will detail how to effectively use Google AdWords. Chapters 11 and 12 will address banner advertising, reasons to use it, banner exchange programs, how to use an affiliate program to get other people to promote your listings, and how they get paid for it. Chapter 13 will cover the important topic of blogging. You will come to understand how much blogging can enhance your image, keep your Web site fresh, and get you recognized as an expert real estate agent or broker in your area. Chapter 14 reveals the new, hot real estate market on eBay, how to advertise on it, and the benefits of an eBay storefront. Chapter 15 covers the topic of when to outsource and how to do it without going over budget. This book also offers case studies of 15 top agents and brokers who have used online marketing, and reveals their secrets and techniques.

1

WHY MARKET ONLINE?

STATISTICS OF INTERNET USAGE FOR REAL ESTATE PURCHASING

Twenty million people are browsing home listings each month. Gone are the days when home buyers would drive around neighborhoods every weekend searching for their dream home. They now have the option of surfing the Web and automatically receiving daily e-mail updates about new homes on the market that meet their exact specifications. This new breed of Internet-savvy home buyer expects more from an agent now than previous generations did.

The statistics of Internet usage for online real estate services are in, and the results are promising. Currently, about 65 percent of consumers use the Internet to search for real estate services, but as more people become aware of the ease and convenience of online real estate Web sites, this number is expected to rise. Also, as online real estate services expand and computer ownership grows, the number of people using online real estate Web sites will grow more rapidly in the next few years.

The top Realtors online are seeing annual sales of four to eight million dollars. How is this possible? They have learned the secrets of aggressive online marketing, and as can happen in traditional business, they have managed to shut out their competition. The process of getting your name on the Internet may seem challenging at first, but using the techniques in this book can lead to recognition of your name and branding so you will gain a reputation as the top person in your field for your local area.

WHAT INTERNET CUSTOMERS WANT MOST

When a consumer decides to start looking at purchasing a home, some may go online first to peruse their local market and see what is currently available. This is a perfect opportunity to win their trust and grab the sale. No one should fool themselves into thinking that personal interaction is no longer a necessary element of online real estate success. A Web site must offer a personal touch and an easy avenue to a local real estate agent by offering contact information and by allowing the consumer to opt for the agent to contact them by phone or e-mail.

Customers want a Web site, with useful features, that helps them through the process of buying or selling property. The great news is, this book is going to show you how to give it to them.

When a potential home buyer goes online to research real estate agents, available homes, and financing options, your Web site should be as close to a one-stop shop as possible. Consumers want to be educated, not just marketed to. There are many first-time home buyers who do not understand the difference between an adjustable rate mortgage and a fixed rate mortgage. What will attract buyers to your Web site is current information about mortgages and interest rates; the types of loans available with major lenders and the pitfalls associated with various loans is valuable information to potential home buyers. They may be first-timers who need to know what principle, interest, taxes, and insurance (PITI) is and why it matters. The most important feature is listings of currently available homes or links to Web sites that provide them. *REALTOR® Magazine* lists multiple listing service (MLS) search capabilities as the number-one and number-two features that consumers want on a real estate Web site. Consumers want to be able to look at all available homes on the market and the market in general. They want to know where the "hot spots" are in their community. Included in this should be features or links that show comparable homes in the neighborhood, current value, and last selling price. Web sites that offer these services such as **zillow.com, trulia.com,** and **buysiderealty.com** are available for you to link to. Zillow offers aerial views of homes, values, and comparable homes and values in the neighborhood. Trulia posts available properties for thousands of agencies and makes its money from ad revenues on its Web site.

Buyers like virtual tours of homes online so they do not waste their time driving to homes that are not specific to their wants and needs. The need for virtual tours cannot be overemphasized. These tours can save your clients a lot of time and also give them the chance to pinpoint what they like and do not like. What should you include in your virtual tours? The number-one feature is the kitchen, followed by the bathroom. Detailed pictures and angles can go a long way toward drawing in buyers. Pictures of the front of the home or condo are also helpful. Be sure to capture the landscaping if the appearance is appealing. Working with your Web designer, you should inquire about all your options, such as 360-degree views of homes for sale. Looking out for consumers and warning them ahead of time about common mistakes in home buying and financing will bring you more business and will increase the chances you will incur goodwill and repeat business. There is no better feeling for a consumer than when they sense an expert is looking out for them. Some other features you should consider for your Web site include a simple mortgage calculator so buyers can get an idea of what type of home they can afford; a brief education into how mortgage loans break down — what is included and what is not; and a printable list of steps first-time buyers can take to work their way toward home ownership, which can bring you business later.

If you still need convincing, here are some statistics. A 2006 poll by the National Association of Realtors asked what service or services consumers want from their real estate agent or broker. More than half of the consumers interviewed said they want help finding the right house to purchase, and in a distant second place, more than 10 percent want help with price negotiations. Almost the same percentage also mentioned they want help with paperwork, want help with information about what comparable homes are selling for, or want help with determining how much they can afford. A mere 2 percent want help finding and arranging financing.

The poll also inquired about the actions taken by consumers who use the Internet in real estate searches. This revealed that 74 percent drove by and/or viewed the home and 61 percent walked through and/or viewed the home online. As you can see, the numbers are impressive, and as computer ownership increases, so will the likelihood that the majority of your new business will be a result of Internet traffic. These statistics confirm that customers online are serious about their inquiries.

USING YOUR EXISTING WEB SITE

If you already have a real estate Web site, now is the time to evaluate keeping your current Web site, designing a new one, or maintaining multiple Web sites. Weighing out the benefits of maintaining one or multiple Web sites is specific to your situation and your plans for growth. Keep in mind that more Web sites can offer you a greater chance of being found online through random searches and offer you a plan to diversify the content to cater to specific clients with different needs or situations. When planning out an Internet marketing strategy, multiple Web sites with links to one main Web site can offer your potential customers a lot of information that links back to you. You can offer all the services home buyers want, and ensure that you have fresh, new features others may not offer, like an online training course in home buying. First-time buyers are a large group of potential customers, so a Web site that caters specifically to educating them can be the service that sets you apart.

Now for the downside: The cost of maintaining your presence online includes monthly hosting fees, changes to the content, adding keywords to your Web site, and fees to resubmit your Web site to the search engines. Obviously, the point of this is to make you more money, but your success is tied to on-the-ground, real-life conditions. If the market in your area is slow, increased Web traffic may not lead to more sales; but in this scenario, even a bare-bones, interesting, and low-cost Web site can increase business enough to make it worthwhile. Also, you have to make the commitment to remain proactive in marketing your Web site. If you are not dedicated to moving your Web site to the top of search engines and updating it on directories, you will probably see only a few leads here and there. One method that has proven to be effective and profitable is pay-per-click. As the advertiser, you would bid for ad positioning on keyword combinations. For example, if you are Chicago's #1 Condo Guy, you would want to bid on "condo sales Chicago" or "Chicago real estate." You may bid on all the keyword combinations pertinent to your business — as many as you like and as often as you like. When a potential client enters one of your keyword combinations, the search will return its results, but with your ad on the right-hand side under "sponsored links."

When someone clicks on your ad, you pay the agreed-upon bid price directly to the search engine. You can specify a daily limit to your clicks so you can control the costs. We will discuss this strategy in greater detail later in the book.

It is helpful if you are part of a large, reputable organization. You should advertise this heavily, as people feel more comfortable trusting someone backed up by established, well-known companies. Starting with an existing Web site that is part of a network offered by a company with solid name recognition is a good first step, but there should be links to more Web sites designed by you that offer services not found on other Web sites. Of course, you can run off your original Web site and enjoy the recognition, but with a combination approach, you can meet the needs of more buyers. Finding market strategies to attract buyers is easier with an established Web site connected to a reputable company, but what if you want to deviate from that or are not part of an established company?

Your image will be further enhanced if you include a photo of yourself, a profile of your real estate experience, statistics or facts and figures about your business, examples of homes that you have sold or are selling, case studies on successful transactions you have made in the past, personal information about yourself, and a light-hearted presentation of your career accomplishments. Testimonials are a helpful resource that will confirm your credibility and establish the trust that you will get the job done for anyone looking at your Web site. Including these little things on your existing page give prospective clients the feeling they know you before they even meet you. And that is a great thing!

Offer a free home valuation to your visitors to the home of their choice. Whether the Web visitors are buyers or sellers, they may be interested in knowing the value of their existing or potential home. Make sure you get all their contact information when they complete the form for their free home valuation. You will learn what to do with this information in a subsequent chapter on auto-responders.

Add new listings on a regular basis, whenever possible. This means you have to get new listings regularly, but hopefully this book will show you how to do that with the help of the Internet. Once you get the new listings, it is your responsibility to make sure you update your Web site immediately. Create a sense of urgency in your listings. Put descriptions that call for action and be descriptive enough to create intense curiosity and interest.

Becoming familiar with SEO, or search engine optimization, is a vital tool for attracting business to your Web site. When buyers go online, it is likely that at least half will go directly to a search engine to start their search. You want to be on the first page that comes up. To do that, you must have information on your Web site that is rich in keywords. Keywords are a critical component for the success of your Web site. Generic keywords are not useful, as search engines will put up millions of matches; so you must locate and use not only keywords, but meta words or meta tags. You should still use the general keywords, but to optimize the chances your Web site will stand out, you must have a variety of key phrases also. Put yourself in the shoes of a home buyer: What would you enter into a search engine? As an expert, your ideas of keywords probably do not match the keywords of a novice. A few examples of words that might be searched on are: realtor, purchase home, first-time home buyer, and mortgage loans. To maximize the chances your Web site will be prominent in a search, you must have Web content matching these keywords. Having articles written that are as rich in keywords as possible while still being educational is your ticket to search engine optimization. You should have a minimum of one page of content for each keyword phrase pertaining to your business. Have articles describing the market or other real estate keywords in every city in which you practice real estate. Bulleted lists of topics or capitalized headlines containing pertinent keywords assist search engines that scan your Web site. Many organizations and writers specialize in researching and writing Web content that is saturated with search engine optimized keywords. If you decide to hire someone, you need to look for companies with a track record of success in search engine placement. While young, hip Web designers may offer creative Web sites, you need standard strategies possessed by experienced companies. Filling your pages with as much information as possible and hooking up the buyer with features once they get there is one available marketing strategy. We will go more in depth on the topics of keywords, meta words, and search engine optimization in Chapters 2, 5 and 6.

Another feature you should display prominently is the past-customer testimonial. Featuring the words of other home buyers talking you up and testifying to their satisfaction makes buyers feel more comfortable about working with you. Also, show the history of your success, such as your sales record and sale times. Do not hesitate to toot your own horn; do not be modest. The purpose of your Web site is to sell you to as many people as possible. Finally, be a member of your community; it only makes sense to have information about your town and the market there versus national real estate information. You should talk up your community, the shopping, the great freeway access, and the nightlife — whatever caters to your niche market. If you want to attract prospective clients planning to move to your area, selling them on the community is a huge plus for you.

BUILDING NEW WEB SITES TO BETTER MARKET YOUR SERVICES

There is nothing more frustrating to a consumer than clicking on an out-of-date or sloppy Web site. Your Web site needs to look professional and offer extensive, timely information. Another irritant is Web sites that force the buyer to enter his or her personal information, which ends up leading to incessant phone calls and e-mails. After spending time on the Web, you learn to avoid these Web sites, as they hound you and probably sell your information to others. This is one of the quickest ways to lose your tech-savvy buyers. An alternative is a weekly or monthly newsletter. This gives the customer the chance to choose to leave personal information in exchange for tips on buying a home, financing, and even fun facts about home improvement. There are other ways to give your visitors the chance to opt for e-mail contact that does not feel forced. If you are going to require that they enter contact information, give them the chance to opt out of repeated e-mails, and have a strong privacy statement. The more information available to your customers, the better, as they will come to you armed with pertinent information, which saves you time spent extracting it from them.

There are many professional Web site development companies that will design and maintain your Web site and help you implement the many features and informative content necessary for an effective Web site. There are important questions you should ask a Web site development company, should you choose to use one. You must inquire about what kind of statistics reports they can offer you. A top-notch service will offer you a report that tells you how many people visited your Web site, how long they stayed, and what features they used. This is important to you, as you can tweak the Web site to correct any weaknesses. Also, it is important to measure traffic so you can tailor the Web site to the audience and know if your keywords are pulling people in. Do they offer an auto-responder? If a prospective client requests more information or a newsletter, an auto-responder will send an e-mail that says, for example, "Hello, you signed up for our newsletter; thanks for your interest." You would then have the option of sending a targeted, personalized e-mail at a later date.

An advanced Web site can offer one of the most popular features: constant e-mail updates of properties matching your client's specifications as they come on the market. This impressive feature takes a lot of searching off your shoulders and the buyer's shoulders. The most confusing aspect of buying a home can be financing, especially for first-time buyers who have no idea what private mortgage insurance (PMI) is or what escrow means. Having a simple explanation of key terms and what to look for when financing a home gives your customers unbiased advice they can trust instead of relying on the financing companies to educate them. One vital feature that should not be taken lightly is contact information. What good is any of this if you cannot communicate with the right people at the right time?

Much additional information is available at your local library and online. Active research for the newest and hottest marketing and Web site tips is a good thing. Do not be afraid to grill your Web host (if you decide to use one) for all the information and tips they possess. You are paying for their expertise, and you should take full advantage of their knowledge and get your money's worth. Ask them what elements they will incorporate into your Web pages that will lead to high positions on popular search engines. What reporting services can they offer you so you know what is working and what is missing the mark? Does the Web site designer offer a guarantee of high placement on search engines? What is their success record? Their goal should be to sell you on using their service.

The art of self-promotion is important to the success of your Web site or sites. You cannot count on directories and search engines. While they are valuable tools, you have to work to get your Web site out there with local advertising. New skills must be learned and mastered that can take you a long way toward making your Web sites work for you. It may seem overwhelming to dive into "keywords" and other online terms, but it is important to your success and worthwhile to your future. Weighing all your options and the cost/benefit analysis is entirely dependent on your goals and growth plans. While the Web is currently an inexpensive place to operate, it will require time and creativity from you, as you know the community you are trying to reach. You can turn over many parts of development and maintenance to experts, but there is no better expert on your brand than you. As we discuss the development of your brand and logo, remember that you need to put them on everything. You are trying to outplay your competition, and doing so requires you to make your brand and logo a household name. The decision lies with you. Only you can weigh all the pertinent facts to decide if joining or expanding with the World Wide Web can offer you enough benefit to constitute the time and money required. You may decide that staying with your current Web site fits your needs, and that is all right. You can always test the waters and add more Web sites if you see the market is there for them. You can still learn valuable lessons about getting business to your Web site, so you can get all you can out of it.

Letting people know you are on their side and you care about their happiness and not just the sale is important. If they are happy at the end and send more business your way, what could be better? It is the hope of this author that this chapter has encouraged the reader to consider maintaining multiple Web sites rich in education, overflowing with features useful to home buyers, and that the reward will be many satisfied customers and a thriving business. Remember, you are the product, and everyone in your community needs to see the benefits of working with you. Now, let us get to work creating a successful brand and promoting that brand everywhere we can think of.

2

CREATING YOUR BRANDING

BRANDING YOURSELF AND DEVELOPING A PROFESSIONAL IMAGE

It is an undeniable truth in the world we live in that no one can or will promote you like you can promote yourself. Branding yourself and putting your name out on the Web requires you to stand out among millions of people and use successful marketing strategies to push your name and your service to the top of search engines and directories. Developing your brand can be a fun process, and you have to decide whether to do it yourself or to obtain professional help. Finding and capturing domain names that fit your branding will help propel your name and your Web site into the forefront of the real estate industry online. Concentrating on a niche in the market and focusing your branding on it is a great starting point for your marketing campaign. When you are an expert in a particular portion of the real estate market, you can make yourself available to television and radio shows and use these opportunities to promote your Web site. A short and simple statement called a "tag line," a memorable logo design, and a dynamic short summary of yourself will tie all your marketing together — domain names, business cards, and print ads. Remember to cross promote your Web site in all print ads, business cards, voice mail messages, and public speaking events. This chapter will cover the development of a brand, name, logo, tag line, and a summary to use in your marketing plan and includes tips on acquiring an easy-to-remember Web site to place on all your marketing material.

Whether you decide to do your promotions yourself or to outsource the job, you should remain in the driver's seat. Your business is the service, and therefore, you must stay actively involved every step of the way. No one knows your strengths and your record better, so speak up and ask for what you want. How does one go about branding oneself? First, you need to look at your strengths, your passions, and what you are known for. Your brand is meant to be an extension of you. Once you have identified the things you want to convey, decide if there is a niche specific to you. Maybe you enjoy the challenge of a tough housing market and can get results when others cannot. That would be a branding point if the market is in a rough spot, but not so much in a boom. This is the whole idea behind branding: translating you into the current market and how that helps the consumer.

You are not going to win everyone over with your brand, but that is all right. You are looking for a portion of the market that will be actively looking for you and potential customers who do not yet know how much they need you.

If this prospect seems overwhelming and you struggle with defining yourself, an alternative is a career coach who can help you answer these questions and assist you in formulating your unique brand. Do not be afraid to add "guru" to your name or "expert;" now is not the time for modesty.

One important issue to decide on up front is whether you want to brand yourself, such as Jane Doe Realty, or if you want to create a branded business that you have created but is not YOU. What this means is you have the option to create a business identity that does not depend on your name for it to survive.

Many successful real estate agents and brokers are realizing that, if they are Jane Doe Realty and they want to retire, Jane Doe Realty ceases to exist. There is no longer any compensation for their years of hard work in creating their brand. Conversely, if a real estate agent or broker creates a brand independent of their name, such as Manhattan Condo Experts, and they are ready to retire, they can sell this thriving business and make money as compensation for their years of creating that brand. Think of this decision as choosing personal fame versus a retirement plan. In the first option, you get to put your name all over your marketing materials and feel important when you become a well-known agent or broker in your local area. With the second option, you may skip the fame associated with having your name splashed everywhere, but have a retirement plan to rely on. Keep in mind, though, choosing the retirement plan option does not mean you cannot still become a known agent in your area. Whether you realize it or not, if you provide an excellent service, people will talk about you, no matter what your business name.

As you formulate and execute your new marketing plan for your Web site that encompasses all possible avenues, remember that your marketing needs to be professional, exciting, catchy, and needs to display continuity so that all your print and online marketing has a unified look. Many companies can design a logo unique to you and help to incorporate your tag line onto promotional materials, such as business cards and other print materials.

Your logo is important, as it is the face of your business and must look good on business cards, letterhead, and other marketing materials. Keep in mind who your target audience is and what would draw them in. It is vital that you share your market focus and business expectations with your logo designer so he or she can design an effective logo. Think about your logo from the point of view of your customers. They see so many real estate agents' ads that you need to stand out. For example, if your specialty is that you can find a house for anyone, even a hard to find house, consider a logo with something like a magnifying glass looking at a house to portray this message. If most agents in your market are using similar marketing materials with logos of a house, consider a logo showing happy customers with a tag line such as "focused on happy customers, not just houses." Remember to make sure your logo and tag line make sense together.

Using color in your logo and business cards can convey more than just pretty hues. Here are the messages people get from colors:

- White: refreshing, pure, light

- Blue: serenity, trust, loyalty, wisdom

- Green: natural, healthy, hope, life, youth

- Black: sophistication, elegance

- Red: uplifting, attention-grabbing

Studies have proven that business cards or letterhead on finer, more elegant paper make a better impression. They offer a more polished, successful look, and offer a good way to stand out from the plain white-card Realtors. It is important that all promotional materials maintain a professional look that conveys you are well put-together and on top of things. If you want to put a picture of yourself on the card, you must determine your audience and dress accordingly. If you want to attract a young, hip crowd, wearing an out-of-fashion jacket is not going to convey youth or give the impression that you are up on the trends.

Most real estate agents and brokers completely misuse their business cards. Your business card provides the opportunity for you to tell the world about what you can do for them, and why you are the best option available. Instead most agents and brokers have their photo taking up the vast majority of their business card. There is no compelling reason why a potential client would choose someone about whom all they know is they are an agent or broker and what they look like.

When designing a business card, think of what the consumer wants, not your ego. Your name, address, and contact info should not be the focal point, but should be the smallest print on the business card. Focus more on listing the benefits of working with you or your company, such as, "We can sell your house in three months or less, even in today's slow market." This way, when someone looks at your card, they are compelled to contact you because of what they know you can do for them. With the average business card, potential customers look at the card and wonder if you can help them. Do not forget, that a business card has two sides. Use the back side that most people leave blank to give your potential customers more reasons and ways to contact you. In summary, use your business card to list your benefits to potential customers.

The Importance of a Short Self-Summary

Deciding on a tag line can be challenging, but worthwhile. Summing up yourself and your professional capabilities in a catchy, short line is difficult for anyone with many successes, but remember this is only the hook for consumers. Once you reel them in, you can make them aware of who you are and what you can offer. Encompassing anyone in a five-word sentence is virtually impossible, but identifying a key strength such as, "I can sell your condo fastest," or "Thirty days for average sale," puts you in the potential buyer's head. Easy to remember, simple tag lines are an advantage for you when others are pushing for a buyer's business. You will have the advantage of being the commercial in their head that will not stop playing. Use the space on your business card to say what you do; for instance, "#1 Condo Seller in

Chicago" with your tag line above — you are saying much while taking up little room on the card. To accompany your tag line and logo, your Web site should show a short self-summary, including what you do. If you meet a potential customer, you should have a short, 30-second summary on what you do and what you specialize in. Create it, rehearse it, and put it on your Web site and all your marketing. This portrays you as a sharp, focused Realtor and will not leave you fumbling or rambling on about ten different, inconsequential facts. You want to draw people in; then you will have the chance to display your accomplishments and strengths. Any successful marketing plan will include all this and display continuity across all forms of advertisement. You want customers to see your logo on any piece of advertising and recognize it as yours. You want to become known as the expert in your corner of the market.

How to Buy a Professional Domain Name

You should spend time online researching domain names for your new Web sites. Looking at other Realtors' Web sites for ideas is a good first step. There is nothing wrong with spying on your competitors' Web sites and seeing what domain names and features are successful. To do this, you will want to view the HTML coding of the Web site. Open up their Web site and click "View" on the tool bar. Once there, click "Source." The window will open and reveal to you the keywords that particular Web site is using to attract traffic. Once you have a list of these keywords, you should run them through the

Yahoo!® keyword selector tool. This will tell you how often these keywords were entered into search engines. On a rare occasion, you may be unable to get the keyword information, but for the most part, it will be right there for you to see.

You want keywords not only on your Web site, but as your domain name. If your niche is condo sales in Chicago, look for domain names that say just that, for example, "chicagocondos.com." A service called Nameboy (**www. nameboy.com**) allows you to enter different combinations of keywords specific to your needs and tells you if they are available. Nameboy does not require membership, and it is free. Not only can you search domain names of interest, but this site will give you ideas to use after entering your primary and secondary keywords.

Not all successful Web sites use keyword domains. As you will be creating a brand, you have the option of creating a unique domain name and marketing it aggressively. Instead of relying on search engines to market your Web site, you can depend solely on advertising to get your Web site into the hands of your prospective customers. If you want to rely on search engine traffic, your domain name must contain keywords that will lead potential clients to you. You want to use the city or community that you serve for the first keyword, and for the secondary keyword, use your identified niche market. Let us say your niche is vacation homes in the Hamptons. Your brand is "the vacation home expert." You would want to acquire a domain name like www.hamptonsvacationhomeexpert. com. If it is available, you can snatch it up. If it is in use, nameboy.com will offer you many alternatives to choose from.

Another tactic to consider is multiple domain names that lead to the same Web site. Domain names are affordable enough that this can be done without considerable cost. This way, every possible keyword combination you can think of that would lead customers to your Web site is covered. Domain names are not the leading factor in search engine rankings, but do matter to an extent. Since multiple domain names that lead to duplicate pages is frowned upon, minor changes to your pages for each domain name will cause search engines to consider them different. Let us say you also want to acquire www.vacationhomeshamptons.com. When someone clicks on your link, it would lead to the same Web site, but with slightly different content.

This is a good time to discuss e-mail contacts to your Web site. You want to be readily available, but at the same time, spam is so prevalent online you may want to limit your inbox to specific addresses like info@ vacationhomeshamptons.com or customerservice@ vacationhomeshamptons.com. These are referred to, in Internet jargon, as your "aliases."

You may see some attractive offers for .net, .us, .ws, or .biz domain names, but you should avoid these, as more respect is given to .com domains. Try to keep your domain names as simple as possible and easy to remember. A free way to get some ideas for domain names is to locate a Webmaster forum and ask the online community for help. This is a great way to get a fresh perspective from people who are not experts in real estate and could have valuable ideas you had not thought of. Also, ask your friends and clients what they think of your domain name or names. Are they asking you to explain the name? If so, keep looking for a better one.

Buying domain names is such an important step that you must take your time and choose wisely. When you find available domain names, you can use Godaddy (**www. godaddy.com**) to purchase them. You can never really "buy" a Web site; you can only lease it for a particular amount of time, which is typically a year at a time. At this point, it is strongly advised that you pay a monthly fee to have a hosting service design, start up, maintain, and run your Web site professionally. So many technical aspects are involved that you need a professional to advise you on all the different options available. This does not mean you exit the process. You are not required to be a computer engineer to know what you want on your Web site. There must be a central computer called a Web server where the files for your Web site are kept. Your hosting service will take on this responsibility, and the fees are reasonable, starting at around $20 a month, depending on the level of maintenance needed. The initial larger fees come when you are first designing and setting up the Web site, as it takes time and effort. Inquire with your hosting companies about registering your domain name on search engines and directories and whether that is included in their fee. Do they have a good search engine optimization track record?

Try to keep your domain names simple, but dynamic. This is another situation in which you want to put yourself in your potential customers' shoes. What would you enter into a search engine if you were starting a preliminary search for a real estate agent? Try out different combinations and see what comes up. The more familiar you are with your competitors' Web sites, the better the chance you can make your Web site stand out. Look at their domain names and formulate a name that sets you apart, but ensures you are easily found online, and that has an easy-to-remember, catchy feel. Ideally, you will be able to find your tag line for use as a domain name, but if not, do not worry. There are millions of keyword combinations, and spending time in front of the computer entering everything you think first-time buyers or consumers would be interested in — for example, condos or summer homes — will lead you to a successful domain name.

Start off with a piece of notebook paper and make a diagram of what you want on your main page, featured items, and what you want on each page. Emphasize to your hosting company the importance of your logo, self-summary, tag line, and other features. This is no time to be modest. Put yourself all over the Web site. Include all your accomplishments, what matters to you, how you want your customers to feel — everything. Tell them you want tons of features and you are willing to link to other Web sites owned by you. There is something to be said for multiple, simple Web sites that link together. Search engines have an easier time finding and listing the pages, and your prospective clients will have faster load times. You need to assess whether you want to offer advertising space to defer some of the costs of maintaining the Web sites. You have a lot of decisions to make, and you will want an expert in your corner.

KEEP ALL MESSAGES THE SAME

How can you maximize traffic to your Web site? As we mentioned in Chapter 1, adding articles is one way. Hiring a writer to keep posting up-to-date, useful content can bring in traffic and keep it there. It is inexpensive to hire a freelance writer to write interesting articles and information for your newsletter. This idea also lends itself to keyword effectiveness. The more varied the content is on your Web site, the more users will find your Web site, as they may approach a search engine with varied questions or searches. Since home buying can be a long process, this is an effective tool, not only to keep prospective buyers hooked, but also to attract buyers midway through the process. You can offer articles on home improvement, financing issues, and general explanations of the home-buying process.

Discuss with your Web designer your need to update content by yourself. Being able to adapt constantly as you get feedback is important to the success of your Web site. Once your Web site is up, you need to spend time there. Make sure you have no "dangling pages," meaning pages that do not link back to you. If a search engine sends a prospective client to that page for their requested information, how will they know you are involved? Is your site easy to move around on? Can your friends and family find the information? Do they find it informative and useful? Are your features operating properly? You should spend quite a bit of time up front on your own Web site, ensuring quality and that you got all that you paid for. It is important that you try to view the Web site through the eyes of a first-time home buyer or whoever your target market is. Some things may make sense to you as a professional, but not to a novice. Do not worry if there are glitches; just keep tweaking things until you are happy and think the Web site or sites will meet the needs of your potential clients.

So, you have your marketing plan, your catchy logo, crisp professional business cards, well-designed letterhead, and your Web site. What now? Now is the time to start putting yourself out there. Contact your local paper for any opportunities to write an op-ed piece on the real estate market, and locate radio stations that offer real estate or business shows that may offer you a guest spot. Look for public speaking opportunities or advertise yourself for public speaking events and do it for free. You will have a captive audience, and displaying your logo, along with marketing materials for everyone, leads to free advertising. If you are good at it, chances to speak and getting paid for it may come along and offer another money-making opportunity. With all these ideas, you will have opportunities to advertise your Web site and your expertise, and you should not hesitate to do so.

Advertising in print media can reach many buyers, especially in specialty sections, like the Sunday "Homes" section. Weekday classifieds are cheaper and will run in the "Homes" section, which is not as elaborate as the Sunday edition, but still worthwhile. Include your entire marketing portfolio, such as your personal summary, logo, and Web address. You can also consider online classifieds or specialty publications, such as apartment rental booklets, that can be found by potentially interested home buyers who do not know how to get started in the process. What better way than to send them to your Web site for information on acquiring financing and credit issues? Educate them on what they need to do to qualify for financing and become homeowners. Offering a feature that helps people now could turn them into customers in the future.

Promote Your Web Site on All Materials

Let us return to the subject of business cards. These little rectangular pieces of paper can hold a lot of information that could lead to great sales. How do you get your cards in the right hands? One way is networking. Locating people in related industries and asking them to display some cards can give you exposure that costs you little. If you know a home inspector or a loan officer, ask them to trade cards with you and do a little advertising trade-off with them. Offer them cash for referrals or a gift certificate for a consultation with you on selling or buying a house. Ask your hairstylist or barber to display your cards and offer to do the same for him or her. Leave a business card when you leave your waitress a tip; 95 percent will get thrown away, but that other 5 percent could find its way to a potential customer. Pin your cards on bulletin boards at apartment complexes, as renters are a great pool of potential business.

The beauty of business cards is that they are cheap, look great, and are easy to carry around. Anywhere you can leave one, leave it. Hopefully, the recipient will look at the card and check out your Web site. Be sure to include a card in all correspondence with personal and business contacts. While I stress throughout this book the effective utilization of search engines, never discount the need to constantly advertise your Web site through business card distribution, voice mail, and print ads.

I have mentioned several times the importance of identifying your "niche" in the market. Here is a list of the top eight niches in real estate: "For sale by owner" properties may not seem like the greatest deal for a Realtor, but many people start off trying to sell on their own. However, once they are exposed to the complexity of the deal, they may change their mind and call you. Resort and vacation homes for those living in vacation areas can be a wonderful piece of the local market. This is a niche that would be greatly served by an Internet marketing blitz. Hispanics are an ever-increasing group of home buyers, and with a median age of 27 years old, they are likely to be a large part of the first-time buyer market in the future. If you can speak Spanish fluently, you should advertise that fact. Retirees and seniors are a niche market that can be a little more challenging and interesting. With varied income levels and special housing requirements, it will stay exciting.

Luxury homes always sound like the best niche, but after the higher-than-normal expenses for advertising, your profits may be the same as lower-priced homes. But for the right people, it can be a great niche. First-time buyers are a large niche market and may need a lot of help. With the requirements of financing and anxieties of the process, they require a little more of you; but in return, you help them get into their first home. If you do a great job, they can be a great source of return business, not to mention referrals. Condos and townhomes offer you the chance to show off your expertise in helping your client find successful investment properties or rentable properties.

Locating your niche does not mean that you are restricted to that market only. It is only for Internet marketing reasons that you offer a Web site for each niche you represent. This targets your message on each Web site to only one group of prospective buyers or sellers. By marketing yourself as the condo expert in Memphis, you come across as being the best person for the job when someone searches for "condos in Memphis." But if you are also helping first-time home buyers, you should have another Web site explaining your expertise in that area. It does not hurt your business or image to have several Web sites — it actually helps a lot.

3

YOUR PUBLIC PROFILE

INCREASING YOUR PUBLIC EXPOSURE OFFLINE AND ONLINE

This chapter will show you how to promote yourself everywhere you go and how to take advantage of all potential marketing opportunities online and offline in daily life. We will cover social networking Web sites, like MySpace, Hi5, and Facebook; writing eBooks; and using forums and blogs to promote your brand and your expertise. In addition, we will explore your options to publish your knowledge in local newspapers and on your Web site.

MEDIA EXPOSURE

Increasing your public exposure offline and online will present opportunities to cover Internet users and those who have not joined the World Wide Web community. By making yourself available and seeking chances to speak on local radio shows or local news shows, you can speak directly to your local community, and it gives you legitimacy as an expert. Most local news shows have occasional real estate segments on their morning shows that offer expert advice to home buyers. They should have no problem with you promoting your Web site — and you should insist on it. There is no shame in promoting yourself, and you should always have the attitude that hiring you is the best thing a prospective client could do. The benefits of working with you are so fantastic that selling yourself makes sense. When you are booked on a television or radio show, issue a free press release online. Later, if a prospective client submits your name into a search engine and views the press release, it gives you an air of legitimacy. List your appearance schedule on your Web site; you can even include an audio or video review of your appearances for prospective clients. When people see you on television, it reinforces your "expert" status — it is impressive.

Contact your local newspaper for any opportunities to write an op-ed piece (sometimes referred to as a "my turn" column). Many newspapers have forms available for submissions that will give you a guide to the format they are looking for. Introduce yourself to local business page editors and let them know you are available for interviews or quotes. Write about the current market conditions and how your clients can still make money. If the market is challenging, bring the positives to light and thoughtfully explain how to overcome the challenges. If the current housing market is booming, speak to your prospective clients about how they can still find a bargain. People like positivity; it attracts people to you and makes them feel good about working with you. Locate local magazines that focus on real estate or on local happenings. Getting your picture and logo on the pages is yet another chance to attract potential clients to look at you a little more closely.

Be Visible in Many Places

Another option is paid print advertising. Most communities have cheap direct mailers or inexpensive newspapers like the *Pennysaver* that reach a lot of people and offer you bargain-basement prices for advertising. Include your tag line, logo, and Web site, and hopefully you will pique their interest enough to check out your Web site and sign up for your newsletter; or at the least, your logo will become more familiar to them. There are so many creative ways to advertise inexpensively that I could not possibly list them all here. Let us discuss a few unconventional offline advertising techniques.

Some companies will pay drivers to put a decal on their car or hand out pens with their business name, logo, and contact information printed on them. Leave your waitress a pen with her tip and a business card, and that pen may end up in the hands of a potential client. Visit the local pubs, get to know some of the customers, let them know what you do, and start a little word-of-mouth advertising. Offer existing customers a referral reward. They send business your way, and you send them out for a nice dinner on you. In every scenario possible, you have a chance to drop a business card and introduce yourself and answer the inevitable question, "What do you do?" This is the perfect time to give your 30-second summary.

Using Forums

Generally, people visit forums looking for opinions or discussions on matters that they want more information on. This means information found in a forum can be used to influence a consumer's decision. Why let this precious opportunity go to waste? Find real estate focused forums or forums for your local area, and periodically write up a post about your services. For example, after an exceptional business transaction, make a forum post on your accomplishment for that client and discuss the benefit you provided them and how this benefit far outweighed the cost. Another suitable forum post is about your knowledge of the national or your local real estate market. If you see trends in your market, write a short post about the trends, where they are going, and how the consumer can take advantage of the situation.

A good way to get started posting in the forums, if you are unfamiliar, is to search Google for real estate forum and your local area, for example "Phoenix real estate forum." Look at the resulting forums for posts from real estate agents. Read them to see what you like and dislike about their posts, and use this knowledge to help you write your own post. In addition, read posts written by non-agents to see what they are looking for. These may provide opportunities to reply to individuals' posts, helping you build credibility with potential clients. Use as many examples of past successes as possible when writing up posts; this further builds credibility with potential clients.

Increasing your visibility online is easier with the advent and popularity of social networking Web sites like MySpace. For the bargain cost of nothing, you can bring friends and family onto your social network page, and they can bring their friends, and so on, and so on. Taking time to create an attractive professional page is key to controlling how people will perceive you. If a potential client locates your page on a search engine and clicks on it, the hope would be that you portray a successful, dynamic person who has many social contacts and links to your business Web site.

In big cities, networking Web sites can be vital to your success. Most of these pages offer a blog section where you can write some articles about your business and successes. This is another opportunity to sell yourself, and MySpace is just one networking Web site to use. Others include hi5, Facebook, and LinkedIn. Linkedin offers a social network that is more business-oriented. It allows you to create a contact network. Each person on your list is called a "connection." Your connections connect to their connections, and so on. You quickly get an expanded list of connections, and therefore, more opportunities to network. You need your connections to introduce you to theirs and vice versa for business networking purposes. There is also an "answers" section where you can respond to real estate questions and become known on the Web site. Facebook and hi5 are similar to MySpace, and are focused more on networking with friends and meeting new people as friends or potential dates. Remember, though, when your friends or their friends look at your page, even though they may be looking at it socially, they will notice whether you could provide them any business services, whether they do so consciously or subconsciously. The more Web sites you register with, the more people will see you, your logo, and your tag line. A few words of warning if you are new to online social networking: This is not the place for hard sales. You must establish yourself as an expert, and slowly encourage people to check out your Web site.

HubPages is not so much a social networking Web site, but it can be of value to you in getting your Web site name out there. You can sign up for free and create a page specific to real estate. Be sure to include the city and state in which you operate. You want to write content that is not sales-related, but is interesting and educational enough that the reader will click on the link to your business Web site for more information. This Web site will allow other community members to rate your article and will let you know how many people have read it. Establish yourself as the go-to person for anyone with a question about real estate.

BE AN EXPERT ON YOUR REAL ESTATE MARKET

We have explained the concept of "appearing to be an expert," but this does not mean you do not need to know your stuff. For everyone to believe in your expertise, you have to know what you are talking about. You should be able to speak about emerging trends, changing conditions, and know statistics to back it all up. If you are able to come up with the necessary time and money, additional schooling would be ideal. Local community colleges or business schools may offer short courses or summer school programs to give you the chance to "refresh" yourself on the topics of economics or business. I should not neglect to mention that it can be challenging for you to "believe" the expert title and thus sell it to anyone else if you are not as knowledgeable as you would like to be. While we are on the subject, offering polls on your Web sites can give you an inside track on the confidence level of home buyers and their mood concerning the current housing market. It also offers a great opportunity to get opinions on features home buyers would like to see on your Web site.

Publish Your Knowledge

Another avenue to consider is writing an eBook. While publishing printed literature requires great cost and many other hurdles, e-books are cheaper to publish and distribute, and often make a little money at the same time. Having "author" added to your list of accomplishments goes a long way toward establishing your name in your community and the market. When you are instructing professionals in your own industry, your name is given more clout in the industry. It is not necessary to write the entire book on your own. You can use a research assistant or a ghostwriter to assist you and save you time. This is one more way to increase your income and offset some of your advertising costs. If you decide an eBook is something you may be interested in doing, decide if you want to write to other professionals or to home buyers. Identify your audience and cater to their specific needs. By knowing your audience, you can formulate a more focused eBook and marketing plan. Let us say you are planning to write an eBook for new home buyers. Besides advertising on your own Web site, it may be worthwhile to pay to advertise your eBook on other Web sites that attract first-time home buyers. With an eBook, you are not bound by city or state lines and can market nationally.

Whether we are speaking of an eBook, Web content, or a newsletter, there are plenty of freelance writing Web sites online that can help you. You can hire good writers at reasonable prices. You offer them the idea of what you want, who you are targeting, and what topics to discuss, and away they go. Of course, you must carefully edit the final document and ensure your Web site and branding is prominent. If you are not comfortable letting someone else do the work and want to do it yourself, have a friend or colleague read it and offer their constructive criticism. One way to do it yourself easily is to write "Ten Tips" articles. Offer an introductory paragraph, ten tips about your chosen topic, and a small conclusion. These are easy to write, easy to read, and, most important, they are memorable.

There are many Web sites on which you can blog or write articles every day. Locate local forums and share what you know with the community you are courting. Educate people on the conditions of the local market, emerging trends, community real estate issues, and anything you think would benefit consumers. While it may not be possible to advertise yourself overtly on these Web sites, listing your name and Web site is certainly commonplace, and could send prospective clients to your Web site to learn more about you. There is a chance you can throw your Web site into your articles if the rules allow it, and if so, you absolutely should. You are probably catching on to a theme here: to shamelessly promote yourself at every opportunity. If done right, no one will know you are doing it. If you are as good as you think you are, no prospective client should be denied the facts of who you are and the benefits of working with you. We mentioned earlier the importance of compelling content on your Web site, and this is extremely important. To maintain absolute professionalism, your Web content, newsletter articles, blogs, and forum entries must be accurate and have no spelling or grammatical errors. The content must be compelling and always display the utmost professionalism and accuracy.

Let us discuss how you can raise your profile in the community in which you will be doing business. Each and every time you deal with a local business and get exceptional service, send a nice letter of appreciation. It is possible they may hang it up for all to see. It shows you support local businesses, and it is the height of professionalism to recognize quality service and products. Local causes or charity events always present you with a chance to be a community leader and get your name out there. It is an accepted practice, and the point is still the charitable cause. There is no better way to put your brand, logo, and Web site out into the community and engender good feelings than to give something back.

When a sale is completed and your clients are in their new home, you should consider dropping off an inexpensive house plant and business cards. Celebrate with them, if just for a moment, and hopefully they will remember the gesture and talk you up to all their friends. Consider taking up a specific cause in your community long-term, like fundraising for a particular charitable group. Your name becomes attached to the group, you get to do something great, and you increase your visibility. Whether your office is located in an outdoor mall or a business park, get to know the people who work around you. They can be good sources of referrals and can direct a lost prospect to your exact location. Take a box of doughnuts over and introduce yourself. Give a business card to everyone you meet and let them know you are available if they ever require your services. Taking care of people takes care of you and your business. You have to deliver on every promise you give to a client or a prospective client. Earning and maintaining a good reputation is too valuable to not do so. Take care of the employees who help you succeed. Not only are they great sources of support, but a great source of referrals as well. Your competitors may try to succeed by running you down, but you should never join in the fight. You will come out on top for the right reasons. Always try to improve your service. Flexibility and self-reflection are the only ways to continually succeed. Now, let us continue with the concept of prospecting.

You should consider direct mail campaigns or e-mail campaigns when your goal is to increase your public profile. There is a fine line between annoying people with too much contact and missing out on letting interested people know you are out there and worth a second look. The answer lies in a multipronged campaign. A direct mail campaign can be an effective way to increase your visibility in your community. The people who receive it may recognize your brand the next time they see it.

There are two kinds of direct mail ad campaigns: your own and one created through a professional direct mailer. The benefit of doing your own is that you are not clumped in with 30 other ads and may stand out more. You may want to avoid purchasing mailing lists, as they can be out-of-date and not worth the expense. The benefit of letting a direct mail company handle your campaign is that they have contact lists already formulated. If you want to send out a mailer on your own, have an assistant start compiling addresses in your local community from the phone book. When you design a mailer, as with all other forms of advertising, include all your marketing tools like your logo, contact information, and Web site. It is a good idea to include interesting statistics so the viewer may stop and read it, and perhaps even save it. As you are well aware, not everyone you attempt to contact is going to be actively watching the real estate market, but if you are creative and get some of them to your Web site, they may sign up for your newsletter. As with all forms of unsolicited contact, you may only snag a few people, but you should know shortly if it is effective.

Some real estate investors use a direct mail campaign that gets an extraordinary response rate using seemingly handwritten letters. There is no reason that real estate agents cannot use similar direct mail tactics. Write the letter by hand, and photocopy it onto paper from a yellow legal pad so that you have several seemingly handwritten letters to mail out. People tend to respond better when they think you took the time to write them a letter. Just be prepared to act like you really did write the letter to each individual when you start to get responses back.

E-mail campaigns are a little trickier. You have to be sure consumers have a way to opt out of future e-mail campaigns. It is vital that you honor unsubscribe requests so you do not get tagged as a spammer. Now seems the ideal time to discuss "netiquette." You should always take care to not contact people too much or with lengthy e-mails. As I am sure you are aware, people are busy. Do not type messages in all caps; this is interpreted as yelling in e-mail. Do not mark messages as "urgent" unless they are. You may fool them once, but next time they will delete your message without even reading it.

When replying to an e-mail, copy and paste some of the original message in case the sender has forgotten what they wrote you about. As with the direct mail method, your best bet is to put out a product that is so interesting and rich in pertinent information, like tips on financing or cheap home improvement ideas, that they will look forward to the e-mail. Offer free consultations by phone; let them know you can help them work on a plan for future homeownership. Too many real estate agents lose interest if you cannot hire them now. There are many people out there who want to buy a home but have credit issues or other hurdles. Giving advice on credit cleanup and financing tips can help them prepare for the future. Offer them a checklist of goals in your e-mail and tell them you will be waiting when they are ready.

4

Online Directories

Listing Your Web Site in Major Directories

When it comes to listing your Web site with various online directories, your choices are plentiful. In the field of real estate, there are countless directories to consider. We will explore the difference between search directories and search engines; what directories can do and what they cannot; and which is better, local or national directories. We will also explore advertising in the Yellow Pages so your prospective clients can let their "fingers do the walking" to locate you online, in the book, or both.

Directories require you to use an entirely different strategy than search engines. While search engines review the content of your Web site to determine placement when a search is performed, directories only take the name of the Web site into consideration. For example, if a prospective client searched "Phoenix real estate broker," a search engine would decide if one of your pages contained relevant information and display it in the results. With a directory, a prospective client would have to click the link to the directory and locate your Web site inside the directory. There is a possibility the search engine would list your Web site inside a particular directory, but not always. This limits you because directories will not consider the content on each page of your Web site, only your domain name. The positive of directories is that, generally, if someone is taking the time to peruse a specialized directory, they are looking for something specific. They know what they are looking for, and are not just browsing.

One of the first steps you should take is finding any and all local directories. You compete with only people in your area, which gives you a much better chance to be seen. If you are an agent working in Phoenix, the best place for you is in a Phoenix directory. Search for your city or area, along with the word "directory," to locate them. Even if a prospective customer's search starts on a search engine, they will likely find their way to relevant directories. This leads us to the conclusion that a dual strategy of registering with directories and optimizing your search engine results is the most likely way to increase your chances of being found online. Combined with the offline marketing of your Web site, you have a good chance of increasing your traffic.

When you submit your Web site for inclusion in a directory, a person will review it and decide if the quality is high enough to be included in the directory and where it will be placed. You will be submitting your entire Web site, not the individual pages. Not as much emphasis is placed on keywords as in search engines, but other criteria are emphasized, which we will address. Some of the major directories to consider are Yahoo! and DMOZ. DMOZ is known as the Open Directory Project and is run by volunteers. The good news is that it is free. The bad news is that it may take a while to get your listing up. While most people do not specifically search DMOZ, Google does. Google gets a lot of information from DMOZ, so take the time to sign up. There is often a backlog due to the large amount of requests and submission errors. Be sure you follow the submission rules to the letter. This directory has the reputation of liking unique content and rejecting Web sites that are not interesting or lack content. If they review your Web site and find dangling pages or it is broken down, they are not going to want you. The Yahoo! directory guarantees a review of your Web site and that it will have your Web site listed within about a week. Unfortunately, it costs about $299. Is it worth it? That is hard to say. The advantages are that search engines will use directory information to assist them in categorizing your Web site, many people use the Yahoo! directory, and when listing your Web site, you may be able to purchase cheap advertising at the top of your category. Last, but not least, the most popular search engine, Google, will take note of the link, and it may help you with placement or page ranking. We will go more in depth on placement and search engine optimization in Chapter 5.

Christopher Sands, of Web consulting firm WebRoyal (**www.WebRoyal.com**), stresses the importance of linking from the major directories: "In order for a search engine to find your Web site, it has to follow a link from somewhere else on the Internet. Directories are a perfect place for this, and search engines routinely scan the directories to find the newest Web sites to add to their catalogue. It's easy, efficient, in many cases *free* . . . and a worthwhile investment in my bag of tricks."

Your second step is to find out if the directory you want to use is indexed on the major search engines. To do this, perform a quick search for the directory in question. Some directories have been banned on the big search engines, and will do you little good if you want the side benefit of increased visibility. Locate the older and reputable directories first, as the search engine Google takes the age of the directory into account for placement. Some search engines get information directly from directories, so it can be a valuable tool to increase your visibility online. Also, having your Web site listed in directories can lead to a higher ranking on the search engines. Some directories charge a fee to list your Web site, but there are free directories as well. Whether or not you should pay for a listing is a hard call to make. You may try starting with the free directories and see what results you get.

When you locate a directory where a submission can be tailored to your industry, there will be a link to click on for submitting your Web site. You should carefully read the requirements and instructions so you will not have to resubmit. Before you submit and subject your Web site to review, you will want your Web site to be running well, have the kinks worked out, and include your logo prominently, as this will increase your chances of being accepted. Your company name must match the title on your home page, and if it is an English directory, your Web site must be in English. When you click the link to submit your Web site, you will likely be given the chance to choose a category. Make sure you read through all the categories thoroughly to ensure you are being placed in the right one. You cannot submit your Web site to two categories in the same directory. The administrator of the directory may not go along with your choice and place you in another category. To better your chances of getting placed in the category of your choice, your Web site must match as closely as possible to the category. Do not hype up your submission by saying you are the "greatest real estate guru who ever lived." You will often not be able to get your Web site listed on that directory. Just give an accurate description of your services and what is on your Web site. Check out any local directories first to ensure it is easy for the community you serve to find you, and move on to national directories.

The reasons generally given for rejecting Web sites for directions are:

- The director does not think your Web site has a professional look.

- The Web site has no real content.

- You have submitted it to the wrong category.

What are your options if a directory does not accept your submitted listing? Sometimes directories get a backlog of submissions due to a personal review of each submission. You should wait at least four weeks, and if you still do not see your listing, send a pleasant e-mail to the administrator of the directory. Give all your information and politely inquire as to the status of your Web site submission. Getting listed on directories can get you listed on other directories for free and without any effort on your part. Users who like your Web site can submit it to other directories they frequent. Consider this the free gift with purchase.

Alexa Internet, Inc. is another tool you should be familiar with. Wikipedia describes Alexa as "a California-based subsidiary company of Amazon.com," and it is recognized for running a Web site that provides statistics on traffic and visitors to other Web sites. Alexa collects information from people surfing the Web and watches to see what page they go to and the subsequent pages they check out. How can this help you? When a person begins a search, Alexa can not only assess the popularity of the Web site, but will guide the user toward other Web sites searched by people with the same interest. If you download the toolbar, you can also get an accurate depiction of the amount of traffic at your Web site and other competing Web sites. You may find some use here, but there are varying opinions on its effectiveness.

Reals.com is a comprehensive real estate directory with every real estate category you could think of. It is a national directory, but it has listings broken down locally. Other directories include **bestrealestatedirectory.com, realestateagencies. com,** and **RealEstateLinksDirectory.com.**

KEEPING COMPANY INFO UP-TO-DATE

Keeping your company information up-to-date on your Web site and all your marketing materials is important.

Out-of-date contact information or old, irrelevant content can give the impression you are off your game. People will not be patient nor should they be. It is imperative that you review your Web site as often as possible and keep it fresh, timely, and accurate. If you are outsourcing the job of maintaining your Web site, you need to keep on top of your provider. You are going to feel the effects, not them. You should also keep your sales record up-to-date and display current positive reviews from your customers to demonstrate your ongoing commitment to your clients. You want to review your Web site often — and this means every page — putting yourself in the shoes of your clients. Check contact information and the flow of the page. Is everything easy to find?

GETTING LISTED IN ONLINE PHONE BOOKS

Listing your business in the online phone books is crucial in several situations. Obviously, if a prospective client wants to look up your number and cannot find it, chances are they will move on to one of your competitors. With the current atmosphere online, many people are "scam ready," meaning they are cynical due to all the scams online. They will investigate you, and if you do not come up in the online white pages, yellow pages, or directory assistance, they may assume you are not a legitimate businessperson. There are many reasons you may not be listed, such as if you use a cell phone or a VoIP (Internet phone system). If you work out of a home office, it can be difficult with a personal home phone to automatically get your work phone listed.

Never fear, you have options. To start, go to the **www. listyourself.net** Web site and sign yourself up. Next, call 411 and search for your listing; if none shows up, call and tell them you are the owner and inquire as to how you can get your listing added. You can do some other legwork as well, but 411 tends to get your number out there for other listings, so this may be sufficient. You can call Verizon Wireless and ask to be put on their "foreign listings," but it comes with a fee and monthly charge. You do not need to be a Verizon customer to use this service. Getting an ad in the Yellow Pages is expensive, but if you work in a localized area, it may make sense to make this investment. If you contact a Yellow Pages representative, he or she can also tell you how often the business category in your area has been searched. Beware of copycat yellow pages — you want the real thing. They also sell services, such as an e-mail link, a detailed information page with features like a map to your location, and information on services offered. Ask the sales representative about signing up for the online Yellow Pages and the paper version.

The biggest positive to using the Yellow Pages is the name recognition. Everyone knows who they are, and most of us, when we are looking for a business, start there. They are respected and generally accurate, though you should be sure to follow up any order by verifying that the ad's content is accurate. Also, submit your information to get listed by the Web site **realestateyellow.com,** since they provide listings for only the category of real estate services.

Several real estate directories exist online and you should seek them all out and get listed in all the free ones and as many of the paid ones as you can afford. A few of them are listed below:

- **NationalHomeSearch.com**

- **RealEstateABC.com**

- **LinkRE.com**

- **Search4Agent.com**

- **RealEstateBest.com**

- **Top-real-estate-agents.org**

- **Remoz.org**

- **GotMyAgent.com**

- **RealEstateIM.com**

- **RealEstatePopular.com**

- **NetSavvyAgent.com**

- **InternationalRealEstateDirectory.com**

- **RealEstate4.com**

- **Reals.com**

- **TotalRealEstateSolutions.com**

There are so many factors you must consider when making your decision about online marketing. It requires you to spend time online researching your competitors and getting an education in Internet marketing techniques and terms. Considering the future of the Internet, you may as well get comfortable with it now because it is only going to become more prevalent. You have to decide whether you want to do the bulk of the marketing work on your own or hire an outside company. The cost/benefit analysis for you depends on your goals and your niche of the market. Obviously if you work in a small town, Internet marketing may not be for you. More traditional marketing methods may be the way to go.

No matter which way you decide to focus your marketing, make a detailed plan, get yourself out there, be memorable, and always take care of your clients. Take every chance you get to meet your neighbors and let them know you are the person to see if they have a real estate issue. Treat all clients like they are the most important people in your life. All the marketing in the world will not help if you do not take care of your customers.

5

UNDERSTANDING SEARCH ENGINES

The best time to ask, "How do search engines work?" is before your Web site is built. This chapter will show you how to maximize your site's effectiveness and earn yourself a top spot in search engine results. We will explore the inner workings of search engines and how Web sites get listed and ranked. How long you will have to wait for your Web site to be listed on the major search engines and whether you should use a free or fee-based Web site search submission site. We will explore these questions and more. The search engines do not advertise how to get to the top of their lists, but luckily for us, many people have solved the puzzle and have shared their knowledge with all of us. It is a constantly evolving entity, so keep an eye out for new strategies. For now we will focus on what is currently known.

HOW DO SEARCH ENGINES WORK?

There are hundreds of millions of pages on the World Wide Web, which is great for all of us. Any topic you can think of will return thousands, if not millions, of hits on a search engine. If you are looking for information on the Internet, this is a boon for you. From a student researching a paper to a consumer comparing real estate brokers in their area, the Internet serves a wide community. So how do you stand out among the crowd? We have already explained the importance of a Web site that has interesting, keyword-rich content, but we will review keywords and the role they play on search engines. We will explore keyword selection in more depth and the tools available to assist you. The Internet is a tricky thing, as is any new technology. It changes so much and so often that keeping an eye on the evolving world of Internet technology is a vital part of your online marketing success. If possible, sign up for e-mail updates on the newest marketing tools available and use them. The need for flexibility in your marketing plan is especially important for search engine results. You should monitor your placement on different search engines and tweak things a little, following the advice I am about to give you. Do not expect instant results from any of the techniques I offer or those listed in the next chapter. It can take up to four to six weeks to see if your tricks are working.

To fully understand search engine optimization or SEO, which we will cover in the next chapter, we need to understand why search engines operate the way they do and why it is secret, why consumers use search engines, and how to operate inside the search engines, using all the tips you can find without crossing the line into an area that may incur penalties. Remember one thing: Search engines want to list you. They want to provide you with good service. Their business depends on the same respect from users that yours does. If you need help, reach out to Google or Yahoo!. Submit questions that respectfully inquire what you can do to improve your rank. If you try everything suggested first, you probably will not need to contact the search engines, but if you are having a problem, do not hesitate to reach out to them. As with any situation, a little kindness goes a long way. The major search engines have a lot of skilled, highly technical staff to help.

Internet search engines like Google, MSN, Yahoo!, and Ask are often the first stop for someone researching a topic online. There are about 206 million users of the Internet in North America, with each user averaging about 77 Internet searches per month according to a ComScore study in August 2007. Most important, 50 percent of the Web community means millions upon millions of people. Your goal is to capture only a small fraction of those users. The opportunities are endless. Even if your main goal is only to attract more business in your community, unexpected opportunities often present themselves once you build up your Web site and have a strong online presence. As revealed in Chapter 3, you can sell eBooks or find other money-making ventures. So hold onto your hat — we are getting ready to get inside search engines, see what makes them tick, and how you can take full advantage of this to put more money in your pocket.

What happens when you enter a keyword into a search engine? The process starts long before you enter a topic of interest. Using automated software, search engines send out "bots" or "spiders" to survey Web pages and use the information to build their databases. These "bots" retrieve the information listed on Web sites and add it to the index of the search engines. They follow each link on each page and survey that information as well. The "bots" survey the text on Web sites and establish what information is contained in the pages.

Obviously, they use shortcuts, as they could not process the information as a whole. They look for repeating words to tell them what each page of your Web site is about. This is why keyword-rich content on each page of your Web site is important. This is just one benefit to keyword-rich content, as you will see.

A keyword is simply any word on any page of a Web site that sums up what your site is about. As the author of your Web page, you can specify the keywords used to identify your Web site, and if you do not, each particular search engine will decide on its own what keywords to use to identify your Web site. Since these searches are automated and not reviewed by a rational human, this software will look for words that are "usually" important. The title of your page gives the "bot" a place to start. Regardless of your strategy to maximize keywords and meta tags, you still ideally want your title to match the content of your page. The algorithm used by search engines will also take this into account and treat more favorably keywords that are used as headlines and that are capitalized. You can also include hyperlinks, which are keywords a client could click on that will lead to information relating to that hyperlink. For example, if this chapter was an article on your Web page, I could make the word "hyperlink" into a hyperlink. If your client clicked on it, he or she would be taken to a page that explains hyperlinks. You can design your page with links that navigate to another page in your Web site with more information.

When writing items for your Web site, remember to keep the copy new, appealing, and pertinent. Many search engines spend a great deal of time and money researching what real, live humans are looking for on the Internet. You can do the same thing by thinking, "What words would I use if I were using a search engine?" Naturally, you want your text to be easy to read and to keep the viewer reading.

Next time you are on the Internet, go to any Web page and, using the tool bar, click on View, then click on Source. A window will open showing the meta tags/keywords used to identify the page you are viewing. Before we get any further into the topic, let us understand what hypertext markup language (HTML) is. HTML is the language your computer speaks behind the scenes. Your browser — whether you use Netscape, Internet Explorer, or Mozilla — is the translator. The browser takes the HTML information and translates it into a Web page for viewing. Meta tags are the HTML code describing the content of each page of your Web site. When you provide these tags, search engines will use the information, and hopefully, accurately designate the content of the pages. While this is only one piece of information the "bots" will take in, it does not hurt to point them in the right direction. You should do anything you can to direct search engines proactively and stay within their accepted practices.

Description meta tags read by the search engine will list a keyword and a small description of your choosing when a prospective client is searching for a service. So when they search "Chicago Real Estate agents," they would come up with not only your Web site or a page on your Web site, but a designated description. You can use this description to pique clients' interests and persuade them to click on the link and go to your Web page. There is an art to writing descriptions that entice the searcher, and if you do not possess that ability, there are free services online that will do it for you. If you want to do it yourself, perform some searches and see how the top-ranked real estate Web sites describe themselves. You can be inspired by their method and write a dynamic description. Use descriptive words and positive self-promotion. You can even use your tag line in the description.

Obviously, you want to use your important keywords as meta tags. You cannot use the same keyword over and over, as this is spamming, and search engine software is smart enough to catch it. This can lead to you being omitted from a search engine. You do not want to use deceptive meta tags just to snag visitors, but you should include common misspellings of your keywords. If you are a "Phoenix Realtor," maybe include common misspellings of Phoenix, such as "Pheonix Realtor." You would not want a chance misspelling to get in the way of a prospective customer locating you. Your would-be customer will find a competitor who took the time to cover this. Yahoo! can provide you with a list of common keyword misspellings to include. You should also include all variations of the keywords associated with your Web site. Make sure the plural version is included. Right now, these are strategies that will benefit you, but the search engine software is getting smarter, so two years from now, this may not be necessary. A common misconception is that meta search engines are related to meta tags, but they are not. Meta search engines simply search other search engines. When you sign up for the big search engines you get the side benefit of being listed on the meta search engines. Now that we have that out of the way, let us talk about "refined searches."

Search engines give users the chance to reduce their search down to the important details. Following the instructions from the searcher, the search engine will exclude or include certain information and hone in on exactly what they are looking for. While a basic search may be "Chicago real estate broker," a refined search may include "condos." This is yet another good reason you want to have many varying keywords that will match as many possible descriptions of your Web page and its content. You have to put yourself into your prospective clients' shoes and think of all the different terms you would enter if you were them. You may want friends or family to help you, as you are so close to the industry you may miss what "regular folks" would enter. Brainstorm and come up with a long list of ideas. Try them out and see what comes up. Remember there are modifiers, like "followed by" and "near" and the terms "or," "not," and "and," that a searcher can use to trim his or her results. Try adding these modifiers to your brainstorm ideas and see where they take you. If a prospective client enters "Chicago AND Realtors," you want that covered in your meta tags so your page comes up in the results. With each page of your Web site you can offer many different meta tags to cover the content. This gives you the chance to snatch top spots no matter what a searcher enters into the search engine.

There are different methods used to refine queries by each search engine, but they have a lot in common. The most helpful tool for you is to read the search engines' help files and apply their directions. How does a search engine decide where your Web site or Web page ranks after someone enters terms relevant to you? How can you use this to your advantage?

Search engines list hits on their results page mostly according to how close they deem the results to match the query entered by the searcher. It is not an exact science, to say the least. The problem with counting on only this is that search engine software cannot reason. It cannot look at your content and make a rational decision about all that is encompassed on your Web site. It cannot see video or hear audio or see your graphics. That means we need to trick them a bit.

This is where keyword-rich content shows its true importance. Though you cannot use repeated terms in your meta tags, you *can* use them to a small extent in your Web content. As you decide what to include in your Web content, whether written by you or by a writer you have hired, it is important that all pertinent terms you want to identify with are repeatedly added. There is an art to writing heavy, dense keyword content, keeping the flow, and keeping it from being "clunky" and obvious. Generally, a good rule is: As long as the content on your Web site is relevant, the search engines are not going to give you a hard time about content and keywords. Do not count on your Web designer to understand this. You have to insist on it and insist on tangible results. If you are not seeing those results, you must change strategies. Before you hire Web designers, interview them thoroughly about their ideas of search engines and how they work. They do not need to know that you already know how they work, but if they give you some simple answers about keywords, move on. You need to hire sophisticated, search engine competent Web designers, as they can design your Web site will all these important facts on their mind.

Different search engines have different keyword requirements to consider. Some want 5 percent of your content to be keywords, while others want a higher or lower density. Some require up to 7 percent to be considered pertinent keywords that they will take into account to index your Web pages. Google only wants 2 percent, so I would recommend staying near that number. Should you try to be all things to all search engines? That is not possible, but trying to please the bigger search engines is worth your time. The major search engines are used by the vast majority of Web users, so you want to concentrate on figuring out how they work and how to improve your chances of achieving a high page ranking on them. Following their guidelines will get you good results on the smaller search engines, especially since many of the small engines are fed by the big engines anyway.

Google is the dominant search engine, and therefore you want to please them so they will list your Web page prominently. Google offers a few peeks into how they work and we need to take full advantage of the help. You can get some general technical information from the Google Webmaster. Just search on the word "Webmaster," and they will provide the link. They have FAQs available on specific topics. They cover a lot, so read as much as you can. They want to list your Web site, but you need to help their "bots" find you and accurately describe your Web site and all associated pages.

You can obtain "crawl info" from Google by following the instructions they provide on the same Webmaster site. This will show you the last time a "bot" from Google visited your page. It will tell you if the "bot" had trouble "crawling" one of your pages and why. This will allow you to fix the problem before the "bot" drops back in. Your Web designer, if you are using one, should be actively involved in this process. Helping you figure out what works, what does not, and how to fix it is part of a Web designer's job. After Google indexes your Web site, they give you the chance to fix any violations and submit a request for re-inclusion of your Web site. Do whatever they ask. They are so important to the success of your Web site that you should cater to whatever they ask of you. What you get in return makes it more than worth it.

You may want to consider blocking some pages of your Web sites so the "bots" cannot crawl them. You should block any pages with internal information that is not for public consumption, like technical pages or pages being worked on. Work with your Web hosting company to accomplish this, although you can do it yourself if you like. It is slightly technical, but some online searching will show you the way.

Some search engines get their information from other search engines; this should help you narrow down which ones to concentrate on. For instance, AOL gets it information from Google; it just presents the information in a slightly different way. It also takes information from the Open Directory Project we mentioned in the last chapter. You do not need to sign up for search engines that do not generate their own indexes. Yahoo! serves the following search engines: AltaVista, AlltheWeb, GoodSearch, and Rectifi. Google serves Compuserve, MySpace Search, Netscape, Mahalo, and AOL. This will save you from wasting time trying to submit to a search engine that does no indexing on its own.

Let us briefly cover the different categories of search engines, as this may come in handy. There are search engines for jobs, news, forums, and blogs, to name a few. You should submit to the blog Web site if you decide to put a blog on your site. There are business search engines you should consider, like ThomasNet (**www.thomasnet.com**) and **Business.com** (**www.business.com**), that serve the U.S. business community. You are probably aware there are property search engines, such as Zillow and RightMove. com (**www.rightmove.com**). You may want to think about adding a link to the property search engines to your Web site. This is only a small sample of available search engines. Just a few minutes searching for them online and you will see many of the options.

What slows down the search engines or will make them notice you for all the wrong reasons? A couple of things have already been mentioned, but it is worthwhile to spend some time communicating this information. We will get into the taboos later in this chapter, too. There are things you can do that dampen the sometimes sensitive spirits of the search engines. As they happily buzz along the World Wide Web, they run into some problems. If you decide to break your Web page into frames, reconsider because search engines have trouble reading them and indexing them, and it can cause unnecessary confusion. To put it simply, search engines by nature index URLs or single pages. When you break pages into frames, you have multiple URLs on a single page. The major search engines are trying to fix this problem, but for now, avoid frames if possible. If someone searches for a topic only contained in one frame of your page and clicks the link, chances are only the framed part of the page will open. It is not that this will get you penalized, but it will not get your page indexed, which is the opposite of what you want.

What makes some search engines better than others? Popularity is one factor. Google is a household name so it attracts more users. Some search engines use the "bots" or "spiders" we explained already, while others use humans to index Web pages. Cha Cha is a search engine that has humans involved in the process. This search engine offers an interesting feature called a "chat interface." If searchers cannot find what they are looking for, they can chat with an employee who will help them find what they need. There is also a new search engine called Blingo that gives away random prizes to their users. This information is presented not because these smaller search engines are necessarily important to your business, but because it reinforces the point that there is always something new out there to consider. If you can get listed in these new search engines, you are not competing with as many other Web sites. Keep your ear to the ground and pounce on these new and exciting ventures.

Do I Use a Free Web Site Search Engine Submission Site?

You now have all the pertinent facts, a killer Web site, and yet you are not listed in the search engines. You have two options: You can submit your Web site free or for a fee.

If you opt to take the free route, it will take longer and there is no guarantee it will work, although it usually does. It may take repeated submissions, but eventually you should get your Web site indexed. You can submit your Web pages over and over again. This generally will not get you penalized because, if resubmission caused removal, people could submit rival pages so they will be removed. So, you can resubmit often without penalty. Whereas if a service attempts several glaringly incorrect submissions or you use software to repeatedly resubmit, you will have a problem.

There are free search engine submission Web sites available. The problem with some of these free submission Web sites is they can make search engines "red flag" submissions made by them. Since it is a free service, you are never quite sure what you are going to get. Not all have the best reputations with the search engines. For a fee, you usually get the assurance of indexing within 48 to 72 hours and repeated indexing every 48 hours. You also get a guarantee that your pages stay indexed on the search engine for the agreed-upon time. There are many people who think paid inclusion is not fair. Starting out, you should stick to the free submissions and just keep at it until your site gets into the search engines, but we will look more at paid inclusion and the benefits in the next paragraph. Here are some submissions pages to get you started with your free submissions:

- Google: **www.Google.com/addurl.html**

- MSN: **www.search.msn.com/msnbot.htm**

- AltaVista: **www.altavista.com/addurl/default**

The one obvious benefit to paid inclusion is that you get a guarantee that your Web pages will be visited often for re-indexing, and therefore, as you add new content, it will show up in the search engines more quickly. You have to pay for each URL, which is each page of your Web site you want listed. Generally, you will be offered a deal to be included in all the paid search engines. For example, for the first URL, you will be charged around $200 a year and about $125 for additional URLs. This can get expensive quickly if you want to include all the pages on your Web site. Also, when the year is up, you are removed from their systems, which, if you had waited, you would have probably gotten on permanently for free.

Some of the search engines that "encourage" paid inclusion are AskJeeves and Inktomi. Inktomi offers a 72-hour turnaround from the time you pay to the time you are listed. They will send out the "bots" every 48 hours to re-index your Web site. They also offer a program called Index Connect, which allows you to submit every URL and lets you dictate the keywords and descriptions. This is similar to a pay-per-click program, though these are generally referred to as "trusted feeds." You provide the search engine with a spreadsheet with the information you want them to use to identify your content. This starts to become close to "cloaking." Cloaking is submitting a different page than the page visitors are sent to. People use this to trick the search engines to increase the traffic to their Web site. Sounds great, but what happens when you break the rules of the search engines? Doing so is never worth it, but before we get to that, a few words on submissions to smaller search engines. If you decide to submit to all who will have you, there is no harm in it. If you have the time, you may see some benefit, but a word of advice: Get a couple of free e-mail accounts and use them when you sign up and verify the inevitable confirmation e-mail, then throw them out. Do not use your personal e-mail or any important e-mail accounts because you are going to get spammed.

Google and other search engines offer paid advertising and other paid services that can make you more visible online. You can purchase an ad and your link and summary will be to the right of the first page of search results. If you are having trouble getting yourself a good page rank after using all the solutions listed in this book, you may want to use this as a temporary fix until you perfect your search engine optimization strategy. The one bonus of these ads is that most users have no idea they are paid ads and assume your site is listed as part of their results.

Earlier we revealed some tricks you can employ with search engines to improve your ranking — there are tricks and there are no nos. The search engines are well aware of the tricks of the trade, and there are a few they do not mind, but others can get your page rank lowered or get you banned for life. The basic way most tricksters try to put one over on the search engines is by using keywords that have nothing to do with the content of the Web site or pages on the Web site. The search engines would prefer that all Web site designers pretend the search engines do not exist. They would like their programs to decide what Web sites and pages are most relevant for specific queries. This is how they were designed to work, but, with increased competition for the top spots in the search engines, they realize they are fighting a losing battle and will let you get away with directing them a bit.

Some other old tricks that are not worth your time are: using irrelevant and unrelated search words, page jacking, and duplicate pages. It is not important for you to know all the technicalities; just make sure you are vocal with your Web designer or host so they know you are not interested in employing these techniques. It is important to stay in good standing with the necessary and helpful search engines, that you use only standard techniques, and that you never build pages that are just for search engine placement. It is possible to get a lot of benefit from legitimate search engine optimization without breaking the rules. We will go into more depth on this topic in Chapter 6.

LINKING FROM OTHER POPULAR SITES

It is time to address the importance of links and how links affect search engines. Search engines take into account the number of quality links you have to other Web sites out there in the World Wide Web. If Google notices the majority of pages that have your links on them are real estate related, you can earn higher placement on their results page. They regard the number of links as a sign you have an important Web site. Also, more links enables the search engines to find your page more easily. No one knows all the factors that increase your pages' value to the search engines, but from what we do know, it is similar to increasing your visibility offline, as we explained in Chapter 3. The more visible you are in the online real estate community, the more the search engines will respect what your page offers. The more links you have to the online real estate community on your page, the higher your page rank from the search engines.

Links can be placed on other people's Web sites to lead Internet users to your Web site. This can be a time consuming process. A good place to start is with friends or business people in your industry. Ask friends with Web sites if they would be willing to link to your site. If you work with a mortgage broker, often you can offer a link trade. You place their link on your Web site and vice versa. Ideally, you want to find popular Web sites to offer your link so you can benefit from their high traffic. If you have employees that are active online in discussion groups or blogs, ask them if they would include a link in their electronic signature. Association Web sites are often quite helpful in promoting those in the industry with links to their Web sites. After some time, you will start to get link requests. If you are using someone's services, like a Web-hosting company, inquire as to whether you can be a "featured client" on their Web site with an accompanying link to your Web site. Send out free press releases online that include a link. They tend to end up producing some results. If you notice your competitors have links on popular Web sites, inquire about adding your link as well. You may want to consider promoting something on your Web site. If you find someone who sells popular real estate eBooks and will list the link and description on your Web site, you get the benefits of their link campaign.

You have to ask yourself whether you want to take on a large-scale link campaign by yourself or take advantage of the many online services who, for a fee, will do it for you. They will assist you in finding and contacting Web sites in your industry with whom you can exchange links. You can link to everyone who will have you, regardless of the ties to the real estate industry, to increase your page rank on the search engines, but that may not always work. Search engines commonly look for quality links, meaning links that make sense. If you have a link on the Budweiser Web site, not only will you not increase your traffic, but the search engine will not consider it. Being in the real estate industry offers you many options for links. From finance and mortgage to moving services, you have enough options that you do not need to look outside your industry. There is no reason that you and any home inspectors or new home builders should not provide links for each other. This serves both of your needs cheaply. A free service online called **linkpartners.com** is a huge compilation of people who want to exchange links with you. This service partners with a paid program called **linkmanager.com** that, after identifying people who want to trade links, does all the work for you. For a service more specialized for real estate, check out **realestatelinkexchange.com.** There are some who will tell you search engines hate this practice, but from what I have seen, as long as they are well run and not random link exchanges, the search engines do not mind.

A little homework can do you a lot of good. Spend time searching for industry related Web sites that come up first in search results. Aim for these Web sites first. In addition to your own search engine placement campaign, you can benefit from their hard work. Contact them and explain why their customers would benefit from working with you and request a link exchange with them. Earlier, we mentioned the importance of content on your pages. Articles not only help you with your search engine placement, they can be reused to acquire additional links. If you give away content to other Web sites with your links embedded in the content, you could acquire a surprising amount of traffic. Imagine you are a Chicago realtor and are writing articles for your own Web site and offer those articles to Realtors in California to use on their Web site. You are not hurting your business by helping them have a more interesting Web site. You get all the benefits of the free links on their Web site. You may be wondering why you would want links on a California Realtor's Web site. Remember links are not always about directing traffic to your Web site, but aiding you in getting a higher position on the search engines.

You have probably seen many of the Web pages you visit offer a "link to us" page. This makes it easier for people to link to you. Do not register links with the "free for all" pages. These are automated directories that let you add your link for free. The result is not increased traffic and the search engine will not recognize these like other links. The only result you get is spam and lots of it. You are required to provide your e-mail address and you will be sorry you did. These "link farms" seem to be in place only to collect e-mail addresses for sale. There may be some who are legitimate, but 99.9 percent of the cases are not worth your time and effort.

Remember our previous discussion about e-newsletters? They can serve many purposes, including providing you with free links and recognition from search engines. When you send out a well-crafted, content rich e-newsletter, it is not the search engine "bot" that will read it. It will likely be placed into Web archives. They actually become Web pages that are indexed by search engines without you lifting a finger. You can also hope the subscribers to your e-newsletter redistribute the content to their own Web sites. As a matter of fact, you should encourage it. If links to your Web site are dispersed throughout the content, these are basically free links to your Web site being circulated without any additional effort on your part. I hope I have convinced you to issue at least a monthly newsletter. The cost and effort is small compared to the dividends they produce, especially considering there are lots of excellent freelance writers available online who will write your newsletters for you cheaply — all you need to do is provide the monthly topics.

BUYING SEVERAL KEYWORD-RICH DOMAINS

We have addressed, in previous chapters, purchasing multiple domain names to cover as many possible keyword combinations relevant to your Web site and pages as possible. How will this affect the search engines and your placement on them? This depends on what you choose. Google will read your URL and take it into account if you apply a basic rule. Say, for example, that your domain name is phoenixrealtor.com and someone enters "Phoenix Realtor" into Google. It will not make the match. It will not see the words in your domain name. A simple fix would be phoenix_realtor.com. This simple separation of the words allows Google to pick up on it and display your page in the results. This can be helpful if it seems all the good domain names are taken. Just add a dash or underscore and you have a winner. Another reason to purchase these domain names is so someone else cannot. This keeps people from benefitting from your hard work. While this provides benefit from Google, you still want your main domain name that is going to be on your marketing material to be as simple and easy to remember as possible. Your other domain names can link to the same page with small differences. Another positive to consider is that some people go straight to their browser bar and enter keyword and add a .com to see what comes up.

After you have purchased your new domain names, you want to ensure they are working properly. When I said before the domain names you choose can all lead to the same Web site, I meant "the same Web site" with a few differences. Remember how we just talked about tricks that search engines do not like? Well, this falls into the same category. For each domain name you have, you should have a separate page that it leads to. Here is one more bit of strange advice: If someone already owns the domain name you want, check to see when their ownership expires; if they do not renew, you can buy it. I am not saying it is worth angering competition, but if they are not using it anymore, anyone can buy it. That is an ethical call you will have to make for yourself. Competition is fierce on the Web so we have to try to keep you one step ahead of the others while maintaining a good reputation, online and off. There are some odd tricks of the trade on the Web, and the great thing is, in discussion rooms, personal Web pages, or blogs, people want to share the secret of their successes and tell you how to avoid their failures. Spending time in technical chat rooms or discussion groups can be as educational as a college class. These people are passionate about the Web and love to spread the joy. We get to eavesdrop and benefit. These are great places to visit when you have technical questions as well.

I mentioned in the last chapter that hiring an assistant can help you spread some of this work around. If you can find a few computer students from a technical school who need work experience, you can take some of the weight of a heavy-duty marketing campaign off your shoulders. If you have an IT guy in your company, ask him for some help. Another word of advice: All the surfing you will be doing and all the information you are acquiring can be a bit overwhelming for anyone. So keep records when you are surfing the Web, because you never know when you will come across a potential Web site you want to link to, or a tip about search engines you will want to remember.

In Chapter 6 we are going in depth on the topic of search engine optimization. Now that you know how search engines work and got a peek into how they decide the ranking for Web pages you should have a pretty good feel for the subject. Check search engines' help files often and you will occasionally get a small hint into how they work. Remember they are not being mysterious for the fun of it. They are trying to keep things fair and keep their competition in the dark about their technical secrets. Try new things and try changing content on your pages, all while keeping an eye on your rank. When we discuss search engine optimization, remember not everything works exactly the same for everyone. Avoid the tricks that annoy the search engines and continue to apply all you are taught and, pretty soon, you will be a real estate expert and an Internet marketing guru.

6

SEARCH ENGINE OPTIMIZATION

WHAT TO INCLUDE AND EXCLUDE ON YOUR WEB SITE

There is nothing more dissatisfying and annoying to a person surfing the Web than visiting a Web site that is out of date. Incorrect information, promotion of events that are past, out-of-date text, and old advertising signify to potential clients visiting the Web site that your time spent updating your site is minimal. Failure to keep your site relevant and up-to-date will undo all the good you are hoping to do with your Web site marketing campaign.

It is not uncommon to search the Internet and find many Web sites with outdated, irrelevant information. Ask any Web design company and they will confirm that they know of at least one or two clients who have not updated their Web site in three years or even longer. Many of these Web sites contain dated information, such as a schedule of events or an old e-mail address. Do not get caught in that predicament. What a waste of time it is to get clients to your site only to show them that you are not interested in providing them timely, pertinent content. Although you may be proud of your Web site and it looks great, if the content is not fresh, it does not take a visitor long to realize the site has not been updated recently and, typically, their interest fades fast.

Even more important is the fact that Google and the other major search engines keep track of how often you update your site, and this factors into how well your Web site does in the search engines. This is referred to as the "freshness" of your Web page content. The search engines check to see if the existing pages have new text, or if you have added entirely new pages or sections to your site. At the least, make sure your front page and major section pages of the Web site are refreshed often with new, relevant content.

Many people outsource this work, and pay a writer to update their Web page with new text daily or weekly, to keep things fresh. Typically, you can pay as low as $5 to $10 each time someone updates the text for you. This is a worthwhile service for such a low price when you consider the positive impact it will have on your Web site.

Conversely, cramming your pages with irrelevant material will prevent the person looking at your site from getting the point of it and understanding the benefits of working with you. Keep your message easy and simple.

Avoid too many flashy text effects. Do not use blinking text, flying text, moving text, or other distracting and dizzying effects — these do nothing more than annoy and distract your visitor. It is best not to create a "loud" Web site that contains so many moving, flashing, colorful, and spinning text, graphics, or icons that people browsing your site are overwhelmed by the effects and disappointed with the site content. Though it is easy to become caught up in the excitement of amusing technology, remember your Web site's purpose is to promote your business on a professional level, not to entertain your site visitors.

Limit the amount of graphics on your Web site so you do not overwhelm your visitors with "graphics overload." It is best not to use animated images on your Web site. These were popular a decade or more ago, but in today's online business environment, they are considered a loud, annoying distraction that site visitors find extremely annoying. Also, keep in mind the type of customer you are marketing to. There may be customers less familiar with using the Web, or those with older computers, and the more flashy, shallow graphics you have, the more you will discourage them from exploring your site, or potentially making use of your business.

Do not use Microsoft FrontPage's themes (the built-in design templates that come with the software) when creating a Web site with this program. Although a lot of computer programmers and Web site designers do not think too highly of FrontPage, the fact is undeniable that it can be used to design good looking, functional Web sites by inexperienced users. Though you can use FrontPage, you do not want your Web site to have the same layout, colors, and scheme as several other Web sites, because this may cause you to lose credibility in the eyes of your site visitors who have seen the same theme on several Web pages.

Do not incorporate frames into your Web site design. If you use frames in one of your Web sites, all parts of the Web site may not be visible to all visitors, and this will drive them away faster than you would think. The search engines often cannot read your Web site if it has frames, diminishing any chance your site may have to obtain a high ranking.

Use the essential Web site design elements already mentioned to make sure your Web site is ready to be found by search engines. The use of search engines has skyrocketed in the past few years, becoming much more popular and easier to use than a phone book or operator system. Be certain your business can be found when a potential customer types in search terms that relate to you and your company's services.

KEEP YOUR MAIN MESSAGE SIMPLE

This is usually the single most important factor that affects and determines your Web page ranking in the search engines. Relevant content on your Web pages is going to increase your Web site in search engine rankings. The text on your Web site is what potential customers visiting your Web site are going to want to read, whether they got to your page by typing it in off your business card or by seeing your site listed in a search engine. It is best to optimize your Web site with good keywords people are searching for so you maximize your rankings in the search engines. You can use several online Web sites or tools, surveys, personal knowledge, or a number of other methods to learn what keywords potential real estate buyers and sellers are typing in when they search on the Internet for houses to buy or an agent to sell their house.

In addition to potential clients and visitors reading the content on your Web pages, search engines are reading the same content and utilizing it to rank the relevance of your Web site among your many competitors. This is why it is important to have the content that search engines look for, so they are able to find your site or sites and rank them near the top of the listings for real estate listings or services in your local area. Search engines troll for key phrases and keywords that categorize your pages, making it vital for you to focus on key phrases and keywords.

Unfortunately, we are no longer able to load up a single Web page with all our keywords, which is sometimes called "keyword stuffing." Google has been tweaked to find this technique, and it hurts your Web site's placement in the search listings in the long run.

When you design the text for your Web site, known as the sales copy, keep in mind that an actual human will eventually read it — not just a search engine. If you were searching for "cure for cancer" in Google, and you found a page that had 1,000 other cures on it, such as "cure for asthma" and "cure for diabetes," you probably would not take the time to wade through all this extraneous information. However, if you found a page that was entirely dedicated to the "cure for cancer" and this page focused on the single topic of cancer, you would be more likely to think the author was devoted to this cure. Do not try to be a jack of all trades. Instead, pick a topic for each page, and focus on this singular topic without trying to stuff in 100 other topics.

Decide on Main Keyword Phrases, and Re-use Them

When it comes to keywords, you need to make an educated guess as to which words or word combinations your potential customers are searching for when they do a search engine query on the Internet. Though this may appear to be one of the easier steps in this process, this could be a large mistake if done without much thought. If you spend your time optimizing your Web site for keywords that potential clients are not searching for, you will wind up wasting your time, and your potential customers will never see your Web site in the top rankings of the search engines. Therefore, you need to do online or offline research to find out what keywords or key phrases are being typed in the search engines to find houses to buy or real estate services in your local area. There are Web sites and software programs available that you can use to find out just what these commonly used keywords are so you can incorporate them into your Web content and use them in your meta tags. In recent years, the importance of the keyword meta tag has faded. Using keywords in each Web page is just as critical as ever and is the key to high search engine rankings.

Search engine optimization simply means every page of your Web site will need to be arranged to get the highest score the search engines can possibly give it. Different keywords should be used on each page based on the content of the individual Web page. If you choose the wrong keywords, you risk not getting seen by any of your potential clients or ending up as a top search result for something completely unrelated to what you are trying to promote. Always keep in mind that, if you are not listed in the top 50 rankings of search engines for important real estate key words, your customers may never find you, and your competition will be getting these potential clients.

You should think about keywords and key phrases for search engine optimization, but you also should think about the exact phrases people use in search engines. Phrases that are too general, like "real estate agent," often get nowhere in the search engines with all the fierce competition, and phrases that are too exact in meaning, like "Chicago's fastest-selling condo agent for 2007," may get no results as well. You need to find a good balance between phrases that get you to the top of the rankings and phrases that get you nowhere. Like most things in life, there is no magic formula for developing search engine optimization and effective search phrases, making this an area in which a professional can make a lot of difference.

The best way to decide on what keywords to use is to determine who your target clients are and think of what they will be searching for when they use a search engine to look for property to buy or an agent to sell their property. Once you determine this, you can better optimize your Web pages. Make sure you use online or offline tools to find out what keywords people are using to find a property to buy or to find a real estate agent. Again, this is an easy yet extremely effective method for increasing your business.

Think of what words you would use when searching for a property or agent on the Internet. But keep in mind, if you rely on your own list of keywords, you will be limiting yourself to using keywords that other people are likely to use. Remember, with your thorough knowledge of your company, the keywords you come up with may be more complex and meticulous than the common potential customer's ideas. Use the available tools to come up with as many keywords and key phrases as possible so you can optimize your Web pages for as many different keywords as possible.

You should have a different list of keywords and key phrases for each page on your site that you are optimizing for the Internet, with the keywords being relevant to the content of each individual page. Keep in mind that keywords that work for some of your Web pages may not be suitable for others. Therefore you should constantly assess how effective your search engine optimization campaign is and make changes if necessary.

An excellent way to keep up with the best keywords is to keep monitoring your competition's Web sites. Use Google and type in some of the keywords and key phrases you know are relevant to search for listings or agents in your area. Take a look at the top-ranking Web sites and see what keywords they use in their site and meta tags. The HTML source code will show you the keywords in the meta tags. You should be able to come up with more keyword ideas from looking at the competition's Web sites, and you will also be able to change your site as necessary so you rank at the top of search engines as well.

KEYWORD-RICH WEB SITE TECHNIQUES

Where you or the designer places certain keywords within a Web page can make a significant difference in your search engine rankings and can become a tricky factor in the success of your marketing. Some search engines analyze only a limited amount of text on each page of your site and, regardless of length, will not explore the rest; therefore, the phrases and keywords you have on your page may not be read by the search engines. While some search engines troll all content, they typically give more "weight" to any content that appears on or near the top of the Web page.

To get the most from your search engine optimization efforts, here are some tips:

1. It may be difficult to put 200 words on some of your Web pages, but you should attempt to get as close as you can. Search engines will give better rankings the more relevant the content seems.

2. Make sure the text on your Web pages contains the most important keywords and key phrases so you will be competitively ranked.

3. Although it is important to incorporate keywords and key phrases, make sure the content containing these keywords is understandable and effective in communicating what you want to say. Many Web site owners get so focused on search engine optimization that they make the mistake of using so many keywords and key phrases that their page is shallow or no longer understandable or readable to the Web site visitor — a sure bet to lose potential customers quickly.

4. Meta tags, ALT tags, head tags, and title tags should be included among your key phrases and keywords on your Web site.

5. Add extra pages to your Web site, regardless of whether they are relevant at the present time. The more Web pages you have, the more pages search engines will be able to link to. Some ideas for other pages you can include are pages with home buying tips, tutorials on how to select a good real estate agent, a case study on a recent smooth transaction you had with a satisfied client, resource information such as good home inspectors or mortgage brokers, and any other additional information you can find that is pertinent to the real estate market in your area.

6. Spread a single keyword phrase throughout the body text. Rather than repeating the keyword phrase many times in the first paragraph, be sure to spread it out evenly between the header, body, and conclusion of the text.

Optimizing your Web pages to make them search engine friendly is the best technique you can use to make sure your Web site is a success. If you are unable to optimize your Web site or are concerned about taking a wrong step, you should hire a professional Web designer so you get the most out of your Web site.

This is the single most important factor that will affect and determine your Web page rankings. It is essential you have pertinent content on your Web site that will increase the site's search engine ranking. The content on your Web site is the first thing visitors see when they find your site and read your Web pages, whether they get to one of your pages directly, from your business card or other marketing material, or from a search engine listing.

Becoming familiar with the concepts and techniques necessary for successful search engine optimization can be confusing when you are first beginning to learn SEO techniques. Once you learn the most lucrative areas to focus on for successful optimization, you will find your ranking in search results will be higher, and your site will get more visitors.

It is critically important that you explore and implement a wide range of tips, suggestions, and known successful practices to give your Web site the highly sought top ranking. The following suggestions may give you more ideas on best practices, tips, and secrets to achieving that success.

Design pages so they are easily navigated by your visitors, because if people can do it, search engine spiders and Web crawlers can too. Search engines prefer text over graphics and also prefer HTML over other page formats. This tip also reinforces the necessity to stay away from too many flashy graphics or animations — this distracts the visitor and is not beneficial to your ranking on a search.

Do not use frames. Search engines cannot easily follow them, and neither can your site visitors. The best advice on frames is simple: Never use them. Limit the use of Flash and other more complicated design applications, as most people get bored with too much fanciness and too little content; plus, search engines have trouble getting any information from them. This could only end up hurting you in search engine listings.

Consider creating a site map showing the location and links of all the pages within your Web site. While this is not the best tool in the opinion of your site visitors, it greatly improves the search engines' ability to properly index all your Web site pages. Make sure all Web pages link back to the main page. Always use copyright and "about us" pages.

Most Web sites use a navigational bar on the left of the page. This is fairly common, but most search engine spiders and Web crawlers will read this before the main content of your Web site. Make sure you use keywords and key phrases within the links in the navigation bar and, if you are using images for your navigational buttons, use the ALT tags with the appropriate keywords or phrases.

Be sure to incorporate keywords into the content of your Web page rather than simply cutting and pasting keywords from meta tags into pages. The search engine views this as spam and, consequently, you will be penalized.

Do not use hidden or invisible text or other tricks designed to fool the search engines. They know these tricks and, if you use them, the search engine could penalize you. For example, do not use text on your Web page that is the same as the page's background color, such as white text listing your keywords on a white background. This technique is known as keyword "stuffing." All search engines are aware of this deception and will detect it and penalize you.

SEARCH ENGINE OPTIMIZATION CHECKLIST

There are several aspects to search engine optimization essential to your online marketing success. We have covered these points in depth already, but having them all in one checklist can be helpful to keep in front of you as you analyze your site.

1. **Title tag.** Make sure your title tag includes the best keywords pertaining to buying or selling real estate in your local area.

2. **Meta tags.** Ensure your meta tags contain all your keywords. Your meta description tag should have an accurate keyword-rich description so potential clients searching the Internet are interested enough to visit your Web site. Do not forget to check for misspelled and plural words in your meta tags, which not only will hinder your rankings, but will look unprofessional and be a turn off to potential customers.

3. **ALT tags.** Images on your Web pages should have ALT tags, which are basically descriptions of the images.

4. **Web content.** Use keywords and key phrases that people will be searching for throughout all your Web pages.

5. **Density of keywords.** Use your keywords and key phrases frequently throughout your Web pages and not just at the top or only on the main page.

6. **Links and affiliates.** Use links and affiliates effectively; otherwise, do not use them at all. Remember to include keywords in your left-hand navigation bar.

7. **Web design.** Make your Web site simple so it can load quickly and is easy for visitors to navigate. You want visitors to read your content, so make sure the site is clean and looks good. It should market your listings and company in a simple way that is informative and should clearly provide your contact information.

8. **Avoid spamming.** Double-check to make sure you do not have any spamming offenses on your site. Some spamming offenses include hidden text, fake doorway pages, overly repeated keywords and key phrases, too many links, and several different pages or sites with the same content.

9. **Keep it fresh.** Frequently update the content on your site and also update the look, feel, and design of your pages periodically to make sure search engines do not think your site is old and not relevant to searches.

OTHER FREE WEB SITE OPTIMIZATION TOOLS

Here are a few more Web design and optimization suggestions that will not cost you anything. In addition, there are some suggested Web sites with useful tools.

Go to **www.Web-Source.net** to get a complimentary subscription to a good e-tips newsletter and to receive a free copy of the eBook *Killer Internet Marketing Strategies.*

Establishing links with reputable Web sites can be free and valuable in your online campaign. You should look for useful Web sites that are compatible and relevant to real estate in your area and approach them for a link exchange. Think carefully about the sites you want to link to; it is not recommended that you link to your direct competitors, such as other real estate agents or brokers in your local area. Link exchanges can get you more visitors and will improve your score with the search engines. You need to be careful not to create a "link farm" or "spam link Web site," where your site has too many links and not enough high-quality content people want to read.

The next free but valuable suggestion is to create press releases for online magazines and newspapers. Another great way to get powerful Web sites to link to your Web site is to create a text press release or an interesting article about the field or industry you are part of. Consider writing an article about your specific market niche and give several helpful tips and techniques for dealing (buying and/or selling) in your industry. When you have completed this press release, submit it to your local and national newspapers and direct it to the person who edits their online edition.

The most important part is to create a byline, which is a short two-sentence paragraph detailing who you are and the link to your Web site. All online publications are required to credit their source and will put your byline at the bottom of the Web page on which they have placed your article.

Learning how to establish a reciprocal link program could

be worth the time it takes in planning. Start your link exchange program by thinking up a title or theme that will be part of your link request invitations; this title or theme needs to be relevant to your site's content. Since most sites that agree to a link exchange will use the title or theme you provide in their link to your Web site, be sure you include relevant keywords, which can help improve your search engine rankings. Keep careful track of your inbound and outbound link requests.

Search for link exchange partners by searching Google for several keyword phrases, such as "link to us," "add your link," "suggest a link," and "add your link." If any of the sites you find are relevant to your real estate site, such as mortgage brokers, loan officers, interior decorators, or home inspectors, you should approach them about exchanging links since they are also online looking for link partners. Make sure the sites that agree to a link exchange with you put a link on their site to your site, since it is common that people do not keep their word and reciprocal links are not made as promised. If they do not link back to you within a few days, remove the links to them from your Web site and look for more possible link partners, since you do not want to be helping them with their search engine rankings if they are not helping you. For it to be fair and worth pursuing, a link exchange needs to be beneficial for both parties. Use **www.linkpopularity.com**, a free resource, to evaluate the total number of sites linking to your site.

The following are more helpful sites:

- **www.websiteoptimization.com/services/analyze**
  Free speed test to show you how to improve your

Web site performance. It calculates page size, composition, and download time. Based on these page characteristics, it offers advice on how to reduce the page load time.

- **www.sitesolutions.com/analysis.asp?F=Form**
  Free analysis of the effectiveness of your meta tags.

- **www.mikes-marketing-tools.com/ranking-reports**
  Offers free, instant, online reports of Web site rankings in the seven top search engines and the top three Web directories.

- **www.hisoftware.com/accmonitorsitetest**
  A Web site to test your Web site for accessibility and usability.

- **www.wordtracker.com**
  The leading keyword research tool. It is not free, but there is a limited free trial.

- **adwords.google.co.uk/select/KeywordToolExternal**
  Suggests new keywords associated with the keywords you provide, but does not indicate their relevance or give details on the number or frequency of searches.

- **www.nichebot.com**
  Tools for Wordtracker and Yahoo!®, along with a good keyword analysis tool, based on Google's results.

- **www.digitalpoint.com/tools/suggestion**

Shows how many searches are done on Wordtracker and Yahoo!® for your keywords of interest.

Telling Google (and Other Search Engines) You Exist

The general guidelines for what you need to consider about marketing your online business are:

Search engines. Make sure you list your Web site with as many search engines as possible, with 15 being a minimum target. There are some sites that are free and some that require a subscription to list your business. Before you decide on either, you need to know that it is possible and easy to manually submit your Web site to Google by visiting **www.Google.com/addurl.html**. Paying to get your site listed quickly in some search engines may make sense, but you will not have to if you can wait for them to find your site. If you can get links to your site placed on a popular site, this will speed up the process of them finding you for free.

Google and other search engines will find your site by following the links from another site. If BarrysAutoFinance. com links to GeorgesAutoService.com, and Google goes to Barry's Web site, it will follow the link to George's Web site.

To quickly get a link from another popular Web site, consider buying one on eBay for a few dollars. By typing in "pr text link" in the search box, you can find established Web sites willing to sell you a link on their site for $10 to $100.

Pay-per-click. There is also pay-per-click and

pay-per-impression advertising. You can read more about these techniques in Chapter 10, where we explore them in more detail and compare them to free advertising options. It is recommended that, for most sites, you should use a paid advertising campaign, and this will also be elaborated on in a later chapter.

Keywords and meta tags. Keywords and meta tags are a small yet important detail in getting visitors to your Web site. Using keywords and meta tags properly can get traffic to your Web site, since search engines use meta tags as part of how they link to and index Web sites. Although meta tags are used by search engines to more accurately list your site, you do not always need them. You can make your Web site without any meta tags and register the domain name with the search engines. Their automated "spiders" or "robots" will automatically index your site based on the content. All search engines function differently, so it is important to understand the subtle differences when it comes to marketing strategies. Experienced Web designers should already know to properly use meta tags.

Generating a High Page Rank

There are no hard and fast rules on how to obtain a high page rank, but if you follow the rules below, you will be well on your way.

1. Only use one meta tag for each type of tag. Using multiple tags for your title is a reason for search engines to penalize you.

2. Do not submit identical pages, subdomains, or domains with identical or similar content with a different Web page file name. Google has been trained to spot duplicate content spread out between many pages. While it seems like you will get duplicate traffic by creating two identical sites with the same content, you will be penalized instead.

3. Verify that every Web page can be reached from at least one link on your main page and your ALT tags for the links are accurate and descriptive.

4. Check for any broken links and that your HTML is correct.

5. Use a text browser — Lynx, for example — to look at your site. You need to see what your site looks like to a search engine crawler. It helps you realize which features, like JavaScript, cookies, session IDs, frames, DHTML, and Flash, are unrecognizable to crawlers and keep them from properly seeing and indexing your entire Web site.

6. Use the robots.txt file on your Web server to alert search engine crawlers to the directories that are or are not available to be crawled. You can find out more about how to properly use this file by visiting **www.robotstxt.org/wc/faq.html.**

7. Have other relevant Web sites, such as mortgage brokers or home inspectors, link to your site. Having others link to your Web site is an extremely important

and easy way of increasing your search engine rankings, though many people seem to overlook this technique.

8. Design your Web pages for people to read, not search engines. You are trying to reach out to the potential customers, not the technology that gets them there.

9. Do not participate in schemes meant to increase your site's ranking using irrelevant or fraudulent links, as your ranking will usually decrease rather than increase.

10. Do not use fake doorway-type pages created for search engines. These are pages automatically generated using fake, filler text that does not have any relevance to your Web site. Most of these doorway page generators use repeated content or content that may be copyrighted. It is dangerous to allow these automated programs to create content for you.

11. Use cascading style sheets (CSS) on your Web site to control the site layout and design. Search engines prefer CSS-based Web sites and typically rank them higher. This is because the design of the site has been removed from the content text of the site, so they are separate. Google in particular loves this technique.

CASE STUDY: E. ROGER BERREY

E. Roger Berrey

E-mail: erberrey@bellsouth.net

Phone: 888-979-9970

"Because experience counts,

call Roger & start packing."

Web Site: **www.OwnTheseHomes.com**

The biggest thing, of course, is that the site must be optimized for top positioning on the search engines. The best Web site in the world is of little value if nobody can find it. The main search engines for consideration are Google, Yahoo, and MSN. If you can effectively optimize for these, you can be very successful in gaining top positioning for your site.

Choose keywords and keyword phrases that you know would be popular entries for customers when they are looking for real estate or a Realtor in your area. Ask your Webmaster to use these keywords when setting up your Web site. You should keep analyzing your site and tracking your progress on a regular basis. Do not expect immediate results, but continue to focus on getting your site on the first page of Google until you succeed.

Also, remember that the search engines can change their algorithms at any time they choose, sometimes affecting your positioning. When this happens, do not panic, but find out why your site is not ranking anymore by going online and researching what they are looking for. It takes work, but with tenacity and a little luck you can get it back up there over time.

CASE STUDY: ROBERT L. SANTANGELO

Robert L. Santangelo, ABR, Broker

Santangelo Real Estate

E-mail: Robert@SoldBySanta.com

Office: 610-993-9990 x222

Mobile: 610-389-3101

Facsimile: 610-993-9985

"Not the Oldest, Not the Largest,

Just the BEST ... SERVICE."

Shop for Philadelphia area homes

at **www.SoldBySanta.com**

In 2002, when I decided to change the focus of our business from the median home price market to a boutique, luxury service firm, the first move I made was to the Internet. Being a heavy Internet user myself, I knew that it was possible to build a brand and establish credibility online. To accomplish this, I felt that a custom site was needed to provide the proper flexibility in both design and content.

I set out to have a Web site that provided value to buyers, particularly relocation buyers. Among other things, our site would give users a database of local shopping, sports, museums, parks, and house hunting ... I even put some games on there. It was critical to make our site "sticky" ... a term used in relation to keeping users on a site. To that end, I was a firm believer in granting access to property searches without requiring registration. There are a couple schools of thought on this topic, but with our philosophy being service-oriented, not sales driven, it was very appropriate. An ancillary benefit of the free registration is that our site generates a minimal number of false leads. Another critical design element of our site was ease of navigation. To this day, the most frequent compliment we get is, "Your site is really easy to use."

Once the site was built, I focused on generating traffic. That led me to the world of SEO. I read all the articles I could find, and I realized that my site, while full of useful information, was painfully lacking in the SEO world ... I didn't

CASE STUDY: ROBERT L. SANTANGELO

even show up when I searched "Santangelo Real Estate"! So, I went through my entire site, page by page, and focused on things like page titles, URLs, meta tags, alt tags, and keyword density — things I had never even heard of. Then, once I thought I had done some good things, I let it sit and the search engines started to reward me. Today, I have high rankings for major keywords that I targeted, but it did not happen overnight, and it took hundreds of hours of time. While I could have hired someone to do the SEO work, outsourcing has never been my strong suit, so the success of our site has given me a tremendous sense of accomplishment. On a monthly basis, we have site traffic generated by more than 800 keywords. Who ever thought it would be interesting to read web server logs?

In summary, I suppose the keys to our Web marketing success can be summarized, as follows:

1. Give users information they want and can use.

2. Create a user-friendly navigation structure.

3. Implement an SEO strategy, and stick with it.

7

BUILDING A NEW WEB SITE

Do you have to be a technology expert, Webmaster, know a lot about Web design, or have extensive online experience to have an effective Web site? The answer is no, you do not. You can learn to use the Internet effectively in a way that will push your business forward, increase the sales of your listings, gain new clients, and promote your business brand to potential customers anywhere who are interested in buying or selling property in your local market. This section will discuss the principles and techniques you can use that will empower your real estate business and Web site to be leaders in online marketing and promotion. Here, we clearly and simply lay out some of the steps you can take to best utilize the Internet to promote and market your listings and your services at little or no cost.

A WEB SITE FOR EACH LISTING WITH A VIRTUAL TOUR

The advantages of creating a separate Web site for each listing are that it will allow buyers to easily peruse each listing and take a virtual tour of the property. Also, if you have the Web site 1234MainSt.com to advertise your listing at 1234 Main Street, it adds tremendous credibility to you. Subsequent pages can be linked that contain the information about the house's statistics and various features. These pages could include school district, directions to or information about the local schools, major points of interests, information about the local economy, and the all-important virtual tour. The virtual tour provides an instant and concise picture of the listing and is accessible at any time, from any location. This saves your buyers time, money, and effort, while at the same time, allowing your company to appear more professional, up to date, and involved with your properties. It also enables potential buyers to make a more effective house search, which leads them to making a better decision in choosing your company. The customer should easily be able to send a link of the virtual tour in an e-mail.

Also, consider, for each of these Web sites for a property, you can link back to your main Web site. By creating many unique Web sites that link back to your main Web site, it forces Google to think your main Web site is important. This is because Google assumes, with so many links to your main site, there must be something important there that everyone is referencing.

A Web Site for Your Blog

Wikipedia defines a blog (a shortened form of the term of Web log) as " . . . a Web site with regular entries of commentary, descriptions of events, or other material such as graphics or video. Entries are commonly displayed in reverse chronological order." The term "blog" is now slang for expressing yourself by writing online or adding content to an existing blog.

There are many blogs that provide commentary or news on a particular subject, such as science, politics, or global news; others function more as an online journal. A blog can combine text with images and links to other blogs or Web pages.

Many blogs have the option for readers to leave comments, which can give you a sense of what your audience thinks of your expertise. We recommend sticking to a blog that, like most, is almost all text, rather than including too many images, videos, or audio. As a busy real estate agent, blogging may seem like another full-time job in addition to promoting your Web site and doing your day job. You can save time by making a successful blog with short posts, if they each contain some nugget of wisdom potential clients would be interested in reading.

A blog will allow you to gain insight into your customers and those visiting your site. This insight can be useful in your marketing strategy, so you can more specifically address the needs and concerns of your target audience.

A Web Site for Finding Buyers Looking for an Agent

To better focus on your customers' needs, you should provide options on the type of agent they want to select. Some buyers will want to do business with a buyers' agent, who exclusively represents the interests of the buyer; however, most agents fall into the category of representing the seller.

If you are primarily a seller's agent but would like to give your site visitors resources on finding good buyers' agents, provide links to the following Web sites or other similar ones:

1. The National Association of Exclusive Buyer Agents exists to support and promote EB as the optimal representation for consumers who want to buy homes (**www.naeba.org**).

2. Directory of Exclusive Buyers Agents for Home and Real Estate Buyers (**www.exclusivebuyersagents. com**).

3. The Buyer's Agent Company specializes in services for home buyers. The site includes information on company, agent profiles, and contact information (**www.ashevillehomebuyer.com**).

The above resources should allow enough selection for a customer to find a buyers' agent if you are primarily a seller's agent. But if you are looking for buyers to show properties to, you can have a specialized Web site made focused on keywords related to buying property in your local area. This Web site needs a lot of specialized information helpful for both first-time home buyers and other buyers, along with reasons why they should let you help them find the right property to buy.

Web Design Mistakes to Avoid

When designing your new Web site, you may be unsure of what to do. Here are some things you should avoid, as they will make your site appear unprofessional or amateurish.

The main page does not quickly describe the focus of the Web site. Any potential customer coming to your Web site should be able to determine the subject of your site in approximately five to ten seconds. This is especially important if you decide to use Flash or another high-volume method of Web design. There are many people on the Web who will not wait even ten seconds for a Web site to load, and if you show a standard "Please wait" message on the front page of your site, it will drive away many people, and they will not get a chance to see your content.

The poor use of pop-up windows, catchy advertising, and splash pages. Too much third-party advertising will automatically take away from your page and become an annoyance to your viewer, as they have to spend time navigating away from the ads to get to the real content. Buyers become impatient if a pop-up window comes up every time they look at a different listing. Keep advertising to a minimum and use links to educate the buyer on other issues related to real estate.

Web site navigational problems. Look out for broken hyperlinks, missing navigation, poorly described navigational links, links that take you to dead-end pages with no links to other pages, and the like. Make your page user-friendly by having a link to your home page from all other pages.

Another useful tool is to add a button to the listing that returns the customer to the original search results.

Do not let your Web site be your marketing campaign or overall marketing and advertising strategy. Remember to advertise in other ways, informing people about the Web site. If the Internet becomes your sole marketing strategy, you will miss marketing to a certain range of customers, and be dependent on your Web site running. If you run an ad in the paper, be sure to place your Web site in the ad and inform the customer to check back often because the site is updated daily with new listings.

Failure to make your Web site relevant with regularly updated content. Nothing is worse to a customer than researching a house that has already been sold. If a builder is no longer running a "no closing cost" special and you advertise it on your site, you will lose credibility and trust. The importance of updating the content on your Web site cannot be over stressed.

Unnecessary text effects. Besides taking a significantly longer amount of time to download your Web page, people can become distracted and not notice the professional content your site is attempting to portray. It can also affect your search engine rankings.

Use a Professional Designer

You can design your Web site entirely by yourself, or you can hire a professional designer to create the site or part of the site for you. In choosing a professional to design your Web site, you need to weigh the time and expense of creating and learning the technology against how much it will cost you to have someone create the Web site for you. If you can do it with confidence, that is great. But if you feel like you need to hire someone, they should show you examples of their work and customer references.

There are numerous high-quality and low-price companies and individuals that perform Web design services. Review our list of Web site design mistakes to avoid and stress the importance of proper Web site design fundamentals to the designer you choose to ensure that all the elements you are looking for are included in the creation of your Web site. Make sure the designer knows your Web site is to be made with search engine optimization and user-friendliness in mind, not just flashiness.

If you have not been trained in graphic design or Web site programming, it will be beneficial for you to hire someone — even if it is a local student in a graphic design program. Your Web site must have a professional appearance and be easy to navigate to be effective. There are hundreds of variables involved in Web site creation, and it will take you years to learn them all. Think of it this way — would you trust a graphic designer with no real estate experience to sell one of your houses?

The good news is that, although this sounds expensive, it does not have to be. Try posting a free classified ad on Craigslist looking for a Web designer to do a simple Web site for you and you will be surprised by how many people will respond with reasonable quotes. There are lots of good Web designers who need experience and are willing to work for a low price if they can use your site in their portfolio.

CASE STUDY: TAMMY BOOKOUT

Tammy Bookout
Broker and owner of VIP Realty Company
8221 Lakeshore Trl W Dr., #2514
Indianapolis, IN 46250
E-mail: Tammy@viprealtycompany.com
Phone: (317) 345 8269
www.viprealtycompany.com

I use a search engine optimization company to do the keyword optimization of my Web site and to do all my online marketing for me. It is expensive, but it is worth it because I get a lot of qualified leads, and it allows me to live the life style I want. Competition is stiff in my area, and I know that in the past the real estate was primarily a referral business, but now with good online marketing, most of my buyers come from out of state. Starting your own business can be scary, but if you spend some money on your online marketing and you do it right, you can get lots of qualified leads. The more money you spend, the more leads you get.

CASE STUDY: DEBBIE RICHARDS

Debbie Richards
Broker and owner of
Debbie Richards Realty Group
E-mail: yourbrokerdebbie@aol.com
Phone: 847-785-0000
www.debbierichardsrealtygroup.com

My Web site has been very instrumental to my business because prospective clients are able to click online for a North Chicago Realtor. Debbie Richards Realty Group was created by Divine Web Design, one of the most phenomenal designers in the Web design business. My business is growing because of my Web site, which also provides valuable information to my clients in addition to the MLS listings.

8

GENERATING WEB SITE TRAFFIC

This chapter describes why you need a form on your Web site to capture potential customers' information, and how to use an auto-responder to automatically contact these prospects and what to e-mail to them.

BUILDING A MARKETING LIST

It is hard work to build a high-quality mailing list. Where and how you get your addresses, how you welcome your subscribers, and how you manage your relationship with your subscribers are vital components of building your list. If you handle these three components well, the relationship can be mutually beneficial to both you and your subscriber for many years to come.

Unsolicited e-mails irritate people as much as the telemarketer who calls at dinner time. Never add an address to your database unless you have the owner's explicit permission to do so. "Permission" means the user has agreed to receive e-mails from you. On the Internet, there are two kinds of permission: "express permission" and "implied permission." As an example, when you have a registration form on your site with a check box that the user can mark to receive your e-mails, that is express permission. The same is true if a user sends an e-mail request to you. On the other hand, implied permission comes when the user clicks on an "agree" button on an end-user's agreement that states e-mail message receipt is a condition of using the site or not removing the check mark from a site registration form that has a pre-checked e-mail permission box on it. Implied permission is another name for "opt-out," and it can be irritating to potential clients.

"Opt-in" is another name for permission e-mail marketing. The two types you should be aware of are:

- Single opt-in: After completing an opt-in form on a Web site or e-mailing a request, the person's e-mail address is added to a list.

- Double opt-in or confirmed opt-in: The individual requests a subscription, which generates an automated e-mail message. If the person does not reply or click a link to confirm the subscription, that person will not be added to the list.

Research shows permission-based e-mail lists deliver better results and cause fewer people unsubscribing, complaining about spam, and blocking your e-mails:

1. Marketers who send unsolicited e-mails with an

opt-out link and then switch to e-mailing strictly to individuals that have opted-in, whether using lists they generated themselves or lists they bought made up of e-mail addresses of people who opted-in, have reported seeing a jump in click rates of about 5 percent. This gets their marketing campaign a click-through rate of 10 percent or even higher in some instances.

2. An IMT Strategies study in 2001 showed how important it is to use permission-based e-mails rather than unsolicited e-mails. More than 75 percent of consumers will delete an unsolicited e-mail without even reading it. Conversely, only 20 percent of consumers are eager or curious to read an unsolicited e-mail, as opposed to 61 percent that are eager or curious to read a permission-based e-mail.

3. A survey taken in 2003 by Harris, prior to the CAN-SPAM law being ratified, found that 79 percent of Americans were annoyed or very annoyed by any unsolicited e-mail — not just the usual spam.

4. People say that they open e-mails from senders they recognize and trust, and delete unopened, suspicious-looking e-mails or those from senders they do not know. In another study, the two main reasons participants said they opened commercial e-mails were because they recognized the sender as something they signed up for (40 percent) and because they recognized the sender's name (52 percent).

5. A study by Quris in 2003 found that people who feel strongly about their privacy and get only high levels of permission-based e-mails are more likely to open and act on those permitted e-mails.

6. Opt-out e-mail list click-through rates are in the range of 1 to 5 percent, while click-through rates on house-generated lists can be 10 to 20 percent higher.

7. E-mail newsletters that use a double opt-in subscribe method have a lower unsubscribe rate of about 7.6 percent compared to single opt-in subscription newsletters, which have an average 22.2 percent unsubscribe rate, according to a 2004 study by AOL.

8. Another AOL study found that their users more often report unsolicited e-mail as spam than opted-in messages. When AOL added the "Report as Spam" feature in the inbox, the percentage of e-mail AOL recorded as spam increased from 25 to 50 percent.

9. Another study showed that more than 70 percent of e-mail users who were offered a spam-reporting button said they use it because they had the impression it would stop them from getting all the unwanted e-mails.

When you send e-mail newsletters or other marketing information to a list of e-mail addresses giving them the option to opt-out, you might be wasting your time. A number of things can go wrong: There may be e-mail addresses that do not exist anymore, addresses that block your messages, blacklisting, and a lack of personal connection with address owners who have no motivation to contact you when they switch e-mail addresses. There are spam-reporting services who create e-mail addresses specifically to add them to mailing lists to see which companies send them spam. Then they report the companies that send these unsolicited e-mails to blacklists or file spam complaints against them. If you get reported several times, if you get plenty of complaints, or if many of your e-mails bounce back due to bad addresses, Internet service providers and e-mail providers may block all e-mails coming from your e-mail address, IP, domain name, or company. To avoid these problems, only send e-mails to customers who have opted-in to get your e-mails.

Capturing Their Contact Information

- **Put a Sign-Up Form on Each Page of Your Site.** Post a link to your registration page every place you meet your customers: on every page of your Web site, in each transactional or customer-support e-mail, and on brochures and business cards.

- **Offer Valuable Benefits.** Newsletters, discounts, contests, special reports, and MLS searches considerably increase the number of people who sign up to receive your e-mails. Promote these benefits on the registration page as well.

- **Optimize Your Site for Search Engine Placement.** Newsletters (current and archived) should also be optimized for search engines; this will lead to increased traffic and subscriptions.

- **Put Your E-mail on the Landing Page.** If you pay for search services like Google AdWords, include your e-mail subscription information on the landing page.

- **"Send to a Friend."** This option can bring you new subscribers with little effort on your part.

- **Include Links in Your E-mail Signature Lines.** Add "Subscribe to Company X's E-mail Newsletter" to your e-mail signatures.

- **Put the Link and a Short Description in All Printed Material.** On business cards, advertisements, flyers, signs, feedback forms, and satisfaction surveys, add "Sign up for our free monthly newsletter at www. companyx.com."

- **Public Speaking Engagements and Seminars.** Promote your newsletter in presentations and handouts, and provide printed copies of your newsletter.

- **Start a Promotional Campaign with a Rented E-mail List.** Advertise your company using e-mail campaigns and squeeze pages, which are pages created to solicit opt-in e-mail addresses.

- **Confirmation/Transaction E-mails.** Add descriptions and links to opt-in pages on all confirmation and transaction e-mails.

- **Promote Yourself in Articles.** Include a reference

and link to your newsletter on articles in trade and consumer publications.

- **Include Newsletter Subscriptions in Lead Generation Forms.** Obtain permission to send your monthly newsletter to trade show booth visitors.

- **Include Opt-in Information on Satisfaction Surveys.** Ask permission to communicate valuable information via e-mail newsletters and promotions.

- **Convey Trustworthiness.** Clearly state your privacy and e-mail policies everywhere it seems appropriate.

You have to work hard to persuade subscribers they can trust your e-mail messages and will find it worth their time to open them. The welcome begins at your Web site's registration page, where you explain your content, frequency, benefits, and so forth, so subscribers know what to expect from you. A good welcome program has these elements:

- A simple opt-in form that requests less information. Ask for only an e-mail address, first name, last name, and preferences in receiving e-mail, in other words if they prefer HTML or text format. At the bottom of the form, you can include an option for details like a phone number and how soon they will be buying a home.

- A thank-you page with additional instructions for the subscriber is essential to finalize the opt-in process. Advise the subscriber that an e-mail confirmation is mandatory to complete the subscription process.

- Send a welcome e-mail to the subscriber that confirms the benefits of the subscription and any other pertinent information. This serves as proof to you that the correct e-mail address was provided and initiates a relationship between you and the subscriber.

- Send a welcome package that verifies the subscriber's opt-in information, a current newsletter sample, detailed benefits of the subscription, links to the preference page, and any other special offers or incentives.

Use the subscribers' e-mail addresses responsibly. The information the subscribers expect from you is what you indicated when they first signed up. The subscribers will quickly unsubscribe if they think their e-mail privacy is being violated.

Tips to Keep Subscribers Happy

Respect the e-mail preferences that subscribers chose on sign up. If you change the type of content, contact the subscribers more often than usual, rent out the e-mail list, or make any other major and noticeable changes to the way their e-mail is used, you will quickly lose your subscribers. The subscribers will remain with you if you stick to your word.

As your e-mail list grows, you must pay close attention to bounces (e-mail coming back), unsubscribes, and any inactivity on your list. In the case of inactivity, send e-mails to reconfirm their subscription and politely acknowledge those who ask to unsubscribe.

Send occasional e-mail offers as a reminder you are still around. Do not overdo it. This will annoy subscribers and they will send you an unsubscribe e-mail.

Get rid of undeliverable e-mails or ones that have not responded to your e-mails

DIRECTING PEOPLE TO THE REGISTRATION PAGE

If you have a newsletter, make sure you have your archived issues available for visitors to view. On this page, you should give them the option of signing up for current newsletters.

Special Articles. Offer your visitors something they can immediately download, such as an article on effective ways to sell their house. They will be more likely to opt in with you if they can get an instant bonus. Consider writing a short article on a topic of importance to your prospects, such as: "Getting $5,000 more for your home." Be sure to create a title that promises specific results, so the user knows what to expect and is more likely to be interested in reading it.

Use a Subscription Link. If you have archived issues of your newsletter, be sure to include a link on all major pages on the site for visitors to subscribe to the newsletter and see old issues.

Address Validation. Make sure potential customers enter their e-mail addresses correctly by using a program that checks for errors when the e-mails are submitted. Below the first box for them to enter their e-mail address, you can add another box that asks them to re-enter their e-mail address to verify it is correct. This will get rid of invalid addresses due to typographical errors.

CASE STUDY: DANIELLE SAYLES

Danielle Sayles, Agent

Speedy Real Estate Services

www.bestrealestateagentchicago.com

In my opinion, the best way to market yourself is to host open houses. Most of the time, the people who come to the open house are not going to buy that house. It is important to be able to keep in contact with these buyers via e-mail as most of them do not have agents.

This is where an auto-responder can be really useful. In order to show them how helpful having an agent is, you should e-mail them a list of other homes for sale in the area that are in the same price range as the home they looked at during the open house. In your e-mail, be sure to let them know that the information and an agent's assistance to help them find a home to buy does not cost them anything. People love anything that is FREE! You should also include first-time buyers' information in the e-mail that helps them understand the process of homeownership. The best part about this way of marketing is, if you have are a loan officer, as well, you can help the prospect and soon-to-be client navigate the deal from finance to close. For this, having an auto-responder send a series of e-mails with all the information mentioned can take a lot of work off your hands so you can focus on what you do best: helping clients buy and sell houses. Ahh, the sweet smell of success!

LEGAL CONSIDERATIONS FOR INTERNET MARKETING

The 2003 U.S. law regulating commercial e-mail, called CAN-SPAM, allows opt-out marketing, but requires a couple of conditions: All commercial e-mails must have properly working unsubscribe functions and e-mails sent to recipients who did not provide "affirmative consent" must include language within the message that it is "a promotional e-mail."

It is becoming more and more difficult to determine what can be called "spam" e-mail marketing and what can be considered legitimate contact. Many Internet operators consider "opt-out" unsolicited commercial e-mails to be spam, but direct-marketing political groups, such as the U.S. Direct Marketing Association (DMA), have put pressure on legislators to legalize such activities. Due to the high quantity of spam e-mail, some users mistake genuine commercial e-mails for spam. Most users rely on spam filters to block unwanted e-mails and, though some marketers complain that their valid e-mails are often caught by these filters, e-mail users are less likely to make such reports.

Several countries have enacted laws against spam, including the U.S. CAN-SPAM Act (Controlling the Assault of Non-Solicited Pornography and Marketing Act) and the European Privacy & Electronic Communications Regulations 2003. Internet providers have also come up with "acceptable use" policies to control spam. Companies that wish to begin an e-mail marketing program must make sure that it does not violate these spam laws. Even so, if Internet mail administrators decide a company is sending spam, the company is likely to be blacklisted.

The CAN-SPAM Act authorizes a penalty of $11,000 per violation, per recipient. Many e-mail marketers in the United States are therefore careful about ensuring compliance with the act, and they employ special services or software to assist them in doing so. Typically, these services require users to verify their return address and include a valid physical address, provide a one-click unsubscribe element, and do not permit the use of purchased lists with addressees who may not have given permission to the company sending the e-mails.

Service providers have also come forward to assist marketers in setting up and managing their own e-mail marketing campaigns. The services they provide include e-mail templates, automatic handling of subscriptions and un-subscriptions, and statistics on the number of messages opened and links clicked on within the messages.

Honor "Unsubscribe" Requests

The most difficult thing you, as an e-mail marketer, must do is comply with unsubscribe requests. You must provide a system in which customers can unsubscribe, and you must make sure they do not receive your future e-mails. If you use a third-party sender, how can you make sure that the senders are honoring your unsubscribe requests? How can you ensure your advertisers are not misusing the suppression list and giving you a bad reputation?

You should make sure your unsubscribe process is simple and works. In every e-mail you send, provide a button that says, "Click here to unsubscribe," or have the subscriber reply with the word "unsubscribe" in the subject line. When someone chooses to unsubscribe, they want immediate results.

Guard your unsubscribe list. Marketers must keep a suppression list for compliance with CAN-SPAM, but many put these names on a Web page or spreadsheet for storage. If spammers steal your suppression list, you will be responsible for its use, and you will be the one in trouble. Always keep the names of unsubscribers encrypted.

Making it easy to unsubscribe does not mean you cannot ask why the person is opting out. Subscribers often choose to end their subscriptions because they receive too many, or they do not believe the messages are personalized or relevant to their needs. Provide a simple form on the unsubscription page for people to state why they no longer want your messages. You can include a checklist of reasons they have for unsubscribing along with an offer to send only specific messages if they stay with you. Take the time to test your unsubscribe system often to ensure that everything works.

The list unsubscribe header is something that marketers can include in messages they send. Recipients will only see an unsubscribe button they can click if they would like to automatically stop future messages.

A list unsubscribe header might look like the following:

> From: kevin@domain.com
> Subject: [espc-realestate] More info on List-Unsubscribe
> Date: August 31, 2006 3:13:02 PM CDT
> To: carol@domain.com
> List-Unsubscribe:<mailto:unsubscribe-espc-realestate-12345N@domain.com>, <http://domain.com/member/unsubscribe/?listname=espc-realestate@domain.com?id=12345N>

Using a header that has a list unsubscribe header in your e-mails will help by reducing complaints, improve the percentage of messages that are delivered, and enhance your subscribers' experience. It is easy to set this up and it costs you nothing. Using a list unsubscribe header is seen as a positive addition to mass e-mails when viewed by most Internet service providers and spam filters, and allows companies that monitor the unsubscribe reputation of mass e-mailers to follow how well you are doing with honoring unsubscribe requests.

Today, a lot of e-mail programs have unsubscribe headers as an option, if it is not automatically part of the program, and other programs let users easily add custom headers. You can make a generic unsubscribe address, but it is much better to use a more tailored unsubscribe e-mail address, such as unsub-listname-1234A@domain.com.

CASE STUDY: DYAN GIRAMONDI

Realtor, Mortgage Broker, Notary
Continental Properties, Inc.
9112 Alternate A1A
North Palm Beach, FL 33403
Cell: 561-307-0400
DyanGiramondi.com

In South Florida (and in many other parts of the United States), it is becoming more and more difficult for realtors to sell their listings in a short time.In order to "entice" buyers and buyer's agents, Realtors have begun to create motivations that seem to be netting results. The most important thing about offering these motivating giveaways is that you have to get the word out about them. For example, if you already have several potential buyers who have looked at a property and you have their e-mail address or their buyer's agent's e-mail, blast out an e-mail with the new deal you are including with the property. And, of course, make sure to put the options into the MLS listing, on your Web site and anywhere else online that you were marketing the property. A few examples of possible options to offer are:

- Offering $1 – 5,000 (or up to all) closing costs to the buyer for the purchase

- Offering Home Owner's Association fees for a time (6 months to one year and more) to the buyer

- Offering a Home Owner's insurance policy for older homes, or newer homes that no longer have Home Owner policies

- Home furnishings such as flat-screen TVs, and furniture that might be desirable to a purchaser

- To the buyer's agent, money is always incentive. Many listing agents offer $1 – 5,000 bonuses to the buyers' agent on its own merit, or sometimes attach criteria such as, if the home is sold by a designated date.

How to Use an Auto-Responder

An auto-responder is a program that sends a response to an e-mail or other inquiry without human involvement. For example, if an e-mail address is no longer valid, an auto-responder will tell you that you have sent an "undeliverable message." Auto-responders can increase your profit by delivering information instantly and following up automatically with your prospects, 24 hours a day. Instead of replying to each e-mail, you can have your auto-responder automatically send personalized responses and follow-up messages.

An auto-responder has the following specific benefits:

- Sends a personalized message to each subscriber in one simple mailing.

- Is able to send e-mail follow ups at any time.

- Sends e-mails on specific dates and times, even when you are not available to send the e-mail yourself.

It takes several contacts with prospects before they decide to give you a chance to work with them. It can be time consuming and manual follow-ups are usually not consistent. An auto-responder makes the follow-up process easier because you are able to respond to clients and prospects much faster and add a personal touch to your e-mails.

Auto-responders will continue to work for you 24 hours per day, 7 days per week. You can arrange to automatically send follow-up messages to your prospects at set intervals without any more help from you, once you set it up.

If you have simple needs, such as sending a single message reassuring your clients or prospects that you will get back to them, you can probably use the free auto-responders that usually come as part of your Web-hosting package. The procedure to set up these auto-responders varies from Web host to Web host, but it is usually as simple as visiting your Web host's control panel to activate it.

If you need an auto-responder to send more than one message or other options, most of these services are offered free in exchange for advertising — that is, advertisements are placed in your auto-responders (usually at the beginning). Visit the following Web sites for more details.

- **Sendfree.com** will provide statistics on how your auto-responder and advertising is performing. Placing free ads on other auto-responders that target your audience is one of the services offered. It is all a numbers game, so when you show two advertisements on your auto-responder, you will have one of your ads displayed on another auto-responder.

- **Freeautobot.com** will send an unlimited number of follow-up messages for you at set intervals that you have decided on and input into the system beforehand.

- **GetResponse.com** also allows you to send unlimited e-mail follow-up messages without considering the length of the e-mail. You are also able to send file attachments with your e-mails, and view the list of new subscribers and statistics. You can configure your auto-responder so e-mail replies are sent directly to you.

Some of the subscribers or clients on your e-mail list may not remember signing up for your e-mails, so at the top of every e-mail message you send out, it is a good idea to put a reminder as to why they are receiving this message, and include a way for them to unsubscribe if they do not want to receive any future mailings from you.

CASE STUDY: TY K. ARRINGTON

Ty K. Arrington, Realtor

Senate Realty Corporation

909 U Street, NW

Washington, DC 20001

202.302.7444 Mobile

202.742.7290 Office

TArrington@SenateRealty.com

www.SenateRealty.com

Once you have a listing, you want every real estate salesperson within a 10-mile radius of the property to be informed about it. The best way to accomplish this is to send out an "E-blast," or reach out to all of these agents through their e-mail. E-mail is one of the best and most utilized tools of a modern real estate agent, but unless you are signed up with an expensive e-mailing service that get these e-mail addresses and sends out the information, it can be quite challenging.

Why the challenge? Many of the more popular named real estate companies that have Web sites have opted to not include their agent's e-mail address on their individual Web sites, but instead give you the option of leaving your e-mail address on their site.

Being the industrious person I am, I found a way to get around this problem. I would simply copy the names of the agents, and then insert their names into the agent finder tab on the Multiple Listing Service (MLS), then press the "e-mail agent" tab that shows up under their name. A new window will open under your e-mail address which will have the agent's e-mail

NEWSLETTER AND E-ZINE CREATION

When you create your own newsletter or e-zine, the most important thing to remember is to deliver them to your designated recipients regularly. The ideal frequency for e-zine distribution is a week. If your e-zine is substantial, you can distribute it less frequently. But if you want to send it more frequently, keep it short and sweet.

Good articles are the most popular content of e-zines. Useful articles help you maintain a good impression with your prospects. They also make for interesting reading material, which is hardly ever available in typical spam e-mails. Having a good set of articles will make your e-mails stand out. Most articles are written in a breezy, readable manner, and are particularly related to whatever your target market is concerned about.

Breakthroughs and updates should also be included in your e-zine. If you have positive testimonials from satisfied customers, by all means, include them as well. Breakthroughs and updates tell your reader you are moving forward at the time of each e-zine distribution. This raises your credibility and appeal.

Q & A or advice columns can give you a lot of free publicity as well. They appeal to readers because you have a section tailored to suit their perspective. Answering questions will help your prospects when they need to voice their concerns and tell you about their needs. You may want to add a link on your Web site where readers can send their questions. This has the added benefit of increasing the hits on your page, as well as providing them an incentive to open your newsletters each time.

Industry news should do more than provide information. It should also include happenings throughout your entire industry. Keeping abreast of the industry and its developments shows you are a reliable source for most prospects. You also make your e-zine versatile with countless benefits your prospects can obtain from it.

Industry news and your role in it can also help you gain leverage when networking with other people in the industry. It also engenders more reaction or feedback from your prospects if you are able to provide general industry news in your e-zine, especially when you are starting out.

Provide space for freebies. People always love freebies, and if they associate your name and your newsletter with good deals and helpful links, this becomes an easy and effective way for you to build traffic. Even without much effort, you will find that people flock in and out of your Web site because you have established yourself as generous and caring.

Whenever you get a bright idea, add it to an article idea list. After a short time, you will have creative ideas for many new issues. Whenever you want to write an article, you can look at your list and choose one of your ideas to write about. Be creative and branch out into other areas. People are more likely to be interested in something that is not the norm.

These days, more and more people participate in forums because they can obtain professional advice for free. This makes forums a great place for you to get useful ideas for your newsletter. Go to the forums where your target market goes, and you will discover many of their most common questions and problems. You can write helpful articles that address these issues.

Discover which keywords your target market is using in search engines, and write an article about that topic. You will not only be providing your subscribers with the exact information they are searching for, but you may also improve your ranking in search engines because of the article, which will bring targeted traffic to your Web site at no cost to you.

Many article directories are available online. You can gain inspiration by browsing categories related to your newsletter topic and looking at article titles. You can get great content ideas for your newsletter this way. Some of the largest article directories include E-zine Articles, Articles Base, Go Articles, Buzzle, and Idea Marketers.

Write how-to articles. You can write these about almost anything, and people love them. Articles that give a certain number of tips are also popular. You can easily think of three tips about any topic and make it into a useful article. Here are some title examples:

- 5 Tips on Choosing a Realtor

- Top 10 Questions to Ask When Buying a Home

- 9 Creative Ways to Get Your House Sold

If your newsletter design is user-friendly and engaging, you will have many more loyal subscribers.

Your readers subscribed for the "content" of your newsletter, so focus on making it easy for them to read and understand. Use a professional yet simple layout that attracts the reader's attention to the text. Do not bother with distracting or enormous graphics that take forever to load on a slower connection.

The first thing you must do is choose the format of your newsletter. The most common formats are HTML, plain text, and PDF.

HTML is becoming very popular. It is a wise format choice because it looks nicer than plain text, and it is a lot easier to make than a PDF document. If you want your newsletter to include photos, images, and other kinds of graphics, HTML is the best format choice.

Often several newsletter designs will look quite different when viewed on different computers or in different e-mail programs. If you do not use an HTML design known to be compatible with all e-mail programs, your newsletter may look like a jumbled mess to most of the subscribers on your list, which will make them unsubscribe or delete it without reading it.

To avoid this problem, you should look at it on several different browsers, such as Internet Explorer, Netscape, and Mozilla Firefox, and test it on several e-mail clients and programs, like Hotmail, Gmail, Yahoo!, Outlook, and Outlook Express, or use a template that has been tested, and alter whatever portions of it you do not like. If you are skilled with HTML design, this is something you can do on your own. However, if you are not familiar with HTML coding and either do not have the time or do not feel comfortable learning it, you can use professionally tested and proven templates.

Plain text can be a practical newsletter format because it is easy and quick to create. You do not have to know how to read or write HTML code and do not need to make a PDF document each time you want to send out a newsletter. Making your newsletters plain text format makes them less likely to be marked as spam than HTML and PDF newsletters. This could save you some hassle and ensure that your newsletters are making it to your subscribers. On the downside, plain text newsletters do not look as professional, and they are not as eye-catching. If the content of your newsletter is the most important thing to you and your readers, using a plain text format will be your best bet.

In the field of Internet marketing, many of the popular newsletters from top experts are sent out in plain text. This is because these experts do not have the time to mess with HTML code to send out each issue of their newsletter.

They prefer to go the quickest and easiest route possible to get their newsletter out and have their audience read it. Their target audience also wants to get it quickly, so everyone involved is all right with having the newsletter published in plain text.

If having your newsletter published in plain text sounds appealing to you, there are plenty of free plain text newsletter formats you can find on the Internet to save you the time of making one yourself.

PDF is less common than the other two newsletter formats, but some people like to use it. It is perfect for newsletters that include several images and have a fancy look to them. If you publish a newsletter with a lot of pictures and graphics in it, a PDF newsletter is a good option for you. However, PDF newsletters can be more time consuming to create because, after you create it, you must convert it to PDF. If you write your newsletter in MS Word and have Adobe Acrobat also installed on your computer, you can quickly convert any Word file to a PDF by clicking Print and then selecting PDF as the "printer." This will save the file as a PDF automatically. Remember, your subscribers will also have to download your newsletter to be able to read it. This extra step will be too much hassle for some people, but if your target reader is more computer savvy and trendy, this may be the perfect option for you.

9

EFFECTIVELY USING YOUR LIST

This chapter shows what to do with the list of prospects you have generated, including learning their needs and generating referrals and recommendations. It also shows how to convert leads on your list into clients.

ASKING YOUR PROSPECTS FOR THEIR THOUGHTS

Asking your prospects for information about them and their needs can help you build rapport with them. Asking questions tells your prospects you care about their situation and gives them the sense that you will consider their needs in the future, and have a desire to create a personal relationship. The more your prospects believe you understand them and their needs (or problems) the more they will want to do business with you. Being able to establish yourself as a trustworthy businessperson, while not talking too much about yourself, helps establish trust and confidence in your abilities. Asking questions, listening, and giving the impression you understand your prospect's situation should be where you spend most of your time; much less effort should go into selling yourself or educating prospects.

As you already know, listening plays a large role in selling your services. In fact, listening is often described as the most important skill in a successful real estate agent or broker's career. Unfortunately, people tend to think listening is the same thing as hearing. Listening is a skill you train your mind to do, which involves actively comprehending the meaning of what a client says and storing what is said in your memory for future consideration. Some tips for improving listening skills are described in the next few paragraphs.

Asking Questions and Knowing Your Prospect

Find out as much as possible about the prospect by asking leading questions and using the information to find the best properties in your listing that suits them. If you get to know your prospects well enough and are able to match their needs to the most suitable property, you will not spend your time showing a list of properties all day long. You will be more productive and helpful to your prospect.

Here are some questions that can help you to learn more about your prospect:

- What type of home do you desire? For example, what would be your ideal style, layout, build, and acreage?

- How many bedrooms and bathrooms are you looking for?

- Have you considered the location? What areas of town would you like me to search for you?

- What are the things that are a must for you that are not negotiable?

- What is your loan approval amount and what amount are you comfortable with?

You can use this opportunity to find out more about your prospect. Ask leading questions that will help you to find out why they want to purchase a home, if they are married, how many children will be living with them, and if they currently rent or own a home. This information is valuable and will help you to learn more about their exact preferences.

Offer support and encouragement to the decisions your prospects make. Make suggestions according to your professional viewpoint, but not before you listen to what they have to say.

Active Listening

It is extremely important you learn how to listen attentively to your prospective clients and current clients. The only way you can assist a buyer or seller is to listen to what they have to say. You will miss pertinent information if you do not listen keenly, and could possibly lose a prospect because of this key factor. Listening attentively enhances your opportunity to build a relationship with the prospect, meet the prospect's needs, and improve the possibility that you will close the sale. Most people are not good listeners since this is not a skill taught in schools. Here are some basic tips and guidelines to follow to hone your listening skills:

- Do less talking. This will allow you to hear your client better.

- Try not to interrupt the client. You do not want it to seem as if your ego is getting in the way.

- Respond in affirmative ways — with a nod of the head, for example — to show you are listening.

- Do not form your own conclusions.

- Do not assume anything. If you are unclear about anything the client says, ask for clarification, with phrases like: "What exactly do you mean by that?"

- Make eye contact and let your body language reveal you are listening.

- Take notes. They can be valuable if you forget anything the client said.

- Do not argue with the client or force your opinion on them.

- Always have an open mind and stay in tune with the client's emotions.

- Make sure you interact with the clients and let them know you understand what they are saying.

- Give your full focus to the client.

CONFIRM YOUR UNDERSTANDING

Paraphrase what you heard the clients say to verify that you understand the message and to avoid misunderstandings. Restate their concerns or opinions in your own words and ask for confirmation of your perceptions. Ask the clients to prioritize their needs so you will have a clear idea of what their most important issues are. This will have the added benefit of helping you remember your client's requirements, and it will help you develop a positive relationship with the client by showing that you are concerned about meeting their needs. Do not repeat every sentence your client says, however, or you may annoy them.

LISTEN TO BODY LANGUAGE

Body language and simple voice inflections can provide clues to your client's preferences, personality, and so forth. A lot of meaning comes through body language, and you can tell a lot about your client's preference for a particular feature or property by keeping an eye on the body language and listening to changes in the tone of voice. If the body language confirms what the prospect is saying, it helps you believe the message. For example, if a client becomes excited when talking about his or her dream kitchen, you know the kitchen is an important selling point for that person. This would also be a perfect chance for you to get personal by asking the client if he or she enjoys cooking and entertaining, thereby making a connection.

On the other hand, potential buyers can tell you one message verbally and something totally different with their body or tone of voice. Body language and tone of voice often give more accurate information than the words people say. When talking with a client, be alert for inconsistencies, like body language that does not match the verbal statements. "Listening" to people's body language can help you translate what they are saying. A client may say a house is "really nice," but his or her body language may shout, "This house is too small."

Clients often get "cold feet" before committing to a property, no matter how perfect the property may be. At this point, you can help them close the deal with the following techniques:

- Remind the client why they originally wanted the property.

- Remind the client of the elements that excited him or her about the house: for example, a beautiful kitchen or garden.

- Highlight the many benefits of the property.

- Help the clients imagine themselves in that space, engaging in family activities.

- Get buyers emotionally involved with the house. People tend to make decisions based on their emotions when buying a home. Justify with valid reasons.

USE THE CLIENT'S OWN WORDS WHEN COMMUNICATING

When you find a certain property you believe meets all your clients' criteria, describe it in the same words the clients used when they told you the type of home they were looking for. This makes it more real for them, as though they were saying it themselves. If you use your own words, you may end up sounding like you are a salesperson. Your words are not theirs, and their words are the only ones that count when they are trying to decide whether to move forward on the property.

This same concept applies to the text on your Web sites. You should use words you have heard your clients use to describe what they want from you rather than your own words. That way, you have the terms that buyers and sellers are searching online with, rather than having words that only Realtors would be searching for. Always remember you are trying to attract more clients and not other Realtors to your Web sites, so keep your words at a client level rather than using industry jargon.

SELLING YOUR PROSPECTS ON YOUR OTHER SERVICES

Whatever your other services may be, your clients cannot use them if they do not know about them. Do you assist with financing or refinancing? Write an article on it in your newsletter. Have you partnered with carpenters or painters? Send out an e-mail stating all the special services you can offer.

If you have partnered with an interior decorator, you may want to keep separate, yearly databases of clients who purchase homes through your services. Keep these databases updated, and after a couple of years, you could send the people on the list an e-mail blast about remodeling services.

Selling Your Prospects on Complementary Services

In your industry, you are bound to come across other professionals with complementary, but not competing, services. For instance, you may know someone who offers a home staging service or a property management company. Think about contacting these companies and making an arrangement where you can get paid for sending business to them. If you sell a house that was custom-built for the client, give them a copy of the subcontractor list and a description of what part each contractor played in building the house. If problems come up and the builder is unavailable, the client will be able to contact the right person to handle the situation.

You can use your list to let your clients and potential customers know about your other services. You gain goodwill from promoting someone other than yourself, and you will gain goodwill from your professional colleagues, who will be impressed you can send them so many good leads.

ASKING FOR FRIENDLY REFERRALS OF OTHER POTENTIAL PROSPECTS

Spreading the word about your business is most often done through word of mouth. Most people, of course, do not recognize or acknowledge this, and the ones who do feel they do not have any control over it. But all real estate agents should agree that word of mouth is the most influential way of advertising. Word of mouth has made or broken more products than all other marketing channels available in business today. Before people trust an article, an advertisement, or even an e-mail, they will trust each other.

It is imperative for your success that you find out what your prospects' thoughts and concerns are. Find out what your potential clients and those who have turned you down are looking for, and how they respond to your information. All marketing requires effective communication to achieve good results.

Why is this important? Because once a potential client has heard about you, visited your Web site, or seen your advertising, they start talking about your services to other people. The prospects' private opinions influence their behavior, but they do not always express how they feel to you. The things they talk about to other people regarding you can influence these people and their acquaintances, and this multiplies in your local area, influencing how well your business does.

Many companies spend a great deal of time and money looking

into how they can effectively use advertising, sales aids, and other promotional materials, which is demonstrated by the fact that you are reading this book trying to learn how to promote your business online. Most people dedicate little time, if any, to researching how word of mouth affects their business. Word of mouth is not static, like a reader visiting your Web site; instead it depends largely on the recipients' questions and on what the speaker has to say. However, just because the person talking about you has an opinion about you, does not necessarily mean their opinion will be conveyed or observed. Questions you should be asking yourself about word-of-mouth conversations pertaining to your business include: What are the nonclients asking the clients? How are the objections, concerns, and fears of your potential clients dealt with? How do your clients persuade their friends to use your services?

Not only should you be interested in hearing what is being said in the free word-of-mouth advertising taking place around you, but you will also want to know the sequence the conversations follow and figure out the source of the information being shared. Do research so you can understand the details in the correct context and sequence. If, during a conversation, the information gets confusing or hard to understand, the person who is confused usually says something like, "Hang on, you're losing me. Can you slow down and go back a little?" When you observe these kinds of phrases in word-of-mouth conversations about your business or any business, it is a sign the marketing message was not successfully passed onto the recipient on the first try.

Having focus group sessions is the perfect way to do word-of-mouth research for yourself because they are the most efficient way to observe the real conversations about your business in person. Focus groups are much more effective than asking clients to remember conversations through which they spread the word about your company, as surveys often ask people to do; instead, you can listen to them directly. Having a focus group session causes real time word-of-mouth communication to occur, rather than mere recall of past word-of-mouth conversations. You can get clients talking with potential clients to help convince them you are the best agent to work with. Right now, you may be saying, "I am a real estate agent, not a marketing researcher!" But this is something you can do easily because it only takes having two or three people together in a room with you, as often happens in your office or at open houses. Learn to take advantage of these situations and openly ask the people gathered together to give you a few minutes of their time to help you understand what people in the community have to say about your services.

In these situations, try out your word-of-mouth research by having focus groups consisting of existing or past clients, focus groups of potential clients, and focus groups of satisfied existing clients combined with potential clients who need convincing. Of course, getting these together will be dependent on the timing and situation, unless you are willing to call people and ask them to meet you specifically for this purpose. When you have them together, ask the expected questions about their opinions and thoughts about your services such as: What information would you share with an acquaintance about me? What questions do you think a highly skeptical person would ask? How do you think you would most likely respond to their objections? Do you feel strongly enough about my services to defend objections?

Conduct another focus group with skeptical people, if possible. Carefully go through the pros of using your real estate service the way it was described to you by the original set of people. Then, listen for the next set of questions and skepticism. Listen to what they say for signs of them becoming convinced, which can be phrases as small as: "Okay, that is interesting, I will think about that." This is a sign their minds are opening. You should then use some of the answers to objections you have previously thought of and some you come up with right there, drawing on your experiences with persuading other potential clients. Try to get them to tell you other objections and reservations they have, since this gives you the opportunity to overcome their objections right away.

Based on your focus group research, you should have learned how to get the advocates of your services to convince the ones who were skeptical. Once you figure out how to achieve that, you will have found the most suitable word-of-mouth messages that you should set as the foundation of your marketing and advertising campaign, including the text on your Web site. Once you have taken the time to do this, your advertising will be tailored to be passed on in everyday conversations. This type of research can take time to prepare and execute, but it could prove to be beneficial to your business in the long run.

KEEPING YOUR PROSPECTS UP-TO-DATE

Maintain a contact list by using contact management software like Microsoft Outlook to keep the most important clients' phone numbers and e-mail addresses up to date so you can keep in touch with them. You can also use a simple spreadsheet program to build a database of clients' contact information. Be sure to keep a backup file on a disk in case your computer crashes or gets damaged in any way. Keep your back up CDs or DVDs in a location other than your office, such as in your home, in a safe, or in a safety deposit box.

If you have lost contact with a prospect, you may be losing business. Keep in touch regularly with your clients so that if there are any changes in their contact information, you will know about it and make the necessary changes to your customer contact database right away. Here are more tips to keep your client contact information as up-to-date as possible:

- **Do not allow anyone else to do your contact updates.** Do them yourself. Make it a personal activity because this is a treasure you want to keep private and personal. When you regularly keep in touch with your customers, you will have the advantage of being able to keep them informed of new listings or services you offer. Updating your contact database may be a laborious job, but it is important. Your prospects or customers are the life of your business.

- **Use electronic devices to store contact information.** Your PDA, cell phone, and iPod can be great tools to use while you are on the go. You will be able to access important information about your client from anywhere. Make sure these devices are synchronized so they have the same contact information. It is likely your devices can be updated and synchronized easily on your computer system.

- **Carefully choose the software programs you use to store your contact list.** The most popular one is Microsoft Outlook. This software was created specifically for contact management, and has unique features to help you maintain and update your database. If you use software programs like Plaxo or GoodContacts, you will be able to communicate with your Microsoft Outlook contact list. Microsoft Outlook will send periodic e-mails to your contacts requesting they verify their information. Some software programs will ask your contacts to update their own contact details. Configure your software to utilize all automatic features that may be available.

10

Pay-per-Click Marketing

Pay-per-click (PPC) marketing is unlike any other form of advertising, online or offline, because the recipient of the ads — not the advertiser or the publisher — determines if and when an ad is paid for. An advertiser can have the highest bids and top ranking for major keywords, but until the prospect clicks and you convert it into a sale, no additional money is made.

You can purchase targeted traffic from a search engine's pay-per-click offers for as little as one cent per visitor. The cost will vary depending on the search engine and keyword. You can open an account with a major pay-per-click search engine for as little as $5, and your listing can be up and running, delivering a stream of targeted visitors, within minutes. You do not need to make any major investment, as you can start by funding your account for a few days and then replace funds as necessary.

The higher the bid you place, the better chance you will have of getting your ad listed at the top of the page. When managed skillfully, pay-per-click advertising can help you attract prospects to your Web site and convert those prospects into clients.

Keep in mind that, just because your ad is highly placed in the "sponsored links" area of the page, does not mean it is effective. It only generates an "impression," which means a searcher has been exposed to your ad — whether they actually see it, read it, or click on it is another story. In most cases, the impression carries no cost because the prospect must click on the ad for you to be billed. However, this does not guarantee a sale or that anyone will visit your site. You need the searcher to click on the ad and go to your site for you to have any chance of getting their business.

WHY PAY-PER-CLICK IS SUCCESSFUL

Pay-per-click advertising is cost-effective, reliable, and, most important, it works. You pay nothing for impressions, so you can use it to test the effectiveness of different keywords, titles, and descriptions. The main reason for the effectiveness of pay-per-click advertising is that you have some control as to where your ad appears. It is successful because you are only marketing to those individuals who are seeking your services, and you only pay when they respond.

HOW TO BUY ADVERTISING

Ad networks sell ads across a number of online sites with a single purchase. This is the easiest place to purchase your advertising. Other options include private advertising agencies, national newspaper Web sites, effective e-mail newsletters, search engines, and sites that specialize in reaching your target audience.

Determine where your target audience is most likely to spend time when online. Those are the sites where you need your ads to be located. It is worth spending more to reach the people who will actually become clients.

Learn the effectiveness of each type of ad. Banners — the advertising boxes that appear on a Web page — are the most common ads, but they are not as effective as other types of ads. Interstitial (or pop-up) ads pop up on a page or interrupt between pages, but can be much more expensive to produce and place, and they can annoy your prospects.

You can also hire an ad agency or designer who specializes in Web advertising to design an ad for you. Pay careful attention to the branding in the message and wording. Be sure to stay consistent with your overall marketing plan so you reach the appropriate audience.

Shop aggressively. The market is competitive, putting you in the driver's seat. You can afford to take a little time to look around at all the deals available and the best prices. You are expected to negotiate the best price for yourself.

Review your results and adjust as needed. Most changes can be made quickly.

GOOGLE

In April 2006, AdAge published a report that Google received a considerable increase in advertising revenues, up $2.2 billion — a 79 percent increase from the previous year. With Google, you can generate revenue from your Web site and obtain immediate exposure to potential clients on one of the most popular Internet search engines. Google offers two different advertising programs: AdWords for advertisers and AdSense for Web publishers.

The Google AdSense program allows Web site owners to earn more revenue from their Web sites by putting up ads targeted to relevant content pages, such as other real estate services. When Google WebSearch is added to the site, AdSense puts up these targeted ads on the side, top, or bottom of the existing pages. The AdSense program pays you money when visitors click on these ads on your pages associated with real estate. It offers enhanced experiences for visitors by including ads that are relevant to what they already see on your pages. The only drawback is that your potential clients may see ads for your competition and go to their Web site instead. You can also add a Google search box to your Web site.

The Google AdWords program reaches people who are looking for information directly related to the real estate or services you choose to advertise, and sends these already interested visitors directly to your Web site. AdWords uses a cost-per-click pricing model, meaning that you pay only when people click on your advertisement. After you pay a small, one-time fee, you will pay for each click on the AdWords ads, which you can control by choosing or changing how much you are willing to pay-per-click with a maximum amount you can spend per day. Google AdWords has a high return rate, and its ease of use makes it extremely popular.

With AdWords, ads for your business appear alongside or above the results on the Google search results pages for Google Web search, along with Google Groups and the Google Directory. Your ads will appear on the right side of these pages and will only appear when a keyword you specified is searched. Ads may also show up on other search sites and on Web sites in the Google Network, an extensive advertising network online. Google's global search network includes the best-known names in online advertising, such as AT&T, AOL, the New York Times, Netscape, Worldnet, CompuServe, AskJeeves, Earthlink, and Shopping.com. Google is affiliated with a network of consumer and industry-specific Web sites sharing content, and members of their network include ABC, USNews.com, TheStreet. com, The Economist, WhatYouNeedtoKnowAbout.com, Thomson, Lowestfare.com, Lycos, InfoSpace.com, National Geographic, Viacom, Forbes, Fox Sports, LinuxWorld.com, and Macworld.

Once you use Google AdWords correctly, your ad will be seen by many people who are looking for specific information about buying or selling houses in your area or about the services you offer. When someone is searching on Google and clicks on your advertisement, they are taken directly to whichever of your Web sites the ad was for. You pay a fixed fee each time someone clicks on your ad, whether the person ever becomes a paying client or not. An important facet of the way AdWords works is that keywords are ranked, so the more desirable or common the keyword, the higher the cost of the click.

After you pay the one time startup fee to join Google AdWords, you will pay for each click from your specific advertisement in Google. It is convenient, however, because you can choose how much you are willing to pay per visitor to your Web site, and you will inform Google of this price when you set up or change your AdWords campaign.

Google AdWords also offers detailed reports and an in-depth hit history to track your ad's performance. It also allows you to change the ad keywords or advertisements to increase visibility and broaden your potential market. Even those who have little confidence in their Web site abilities usually do not need to hire a professional to manage their Google AdWords campaign because it is simple to set up and monitor, though some Web site owners choose to hire a professional to manage their AdWords campaign because the professionals have more experience and time to dedicate to the project. This allows them to quickly tweak the ads and bids to obtain a high click-through rate.

Google has online tutorials that are divided into small, easily understood sections, which you can go through before you decide if you want to create an account. Google AdWords works differently than most pay-per-click companies. Along with the dollar value, you bid for your keywords of interest. Other factors are important in deciding how close to the top your ad is placed, such as how good they think the quality of your Web site is. This is all explained in the tutorial available on their Web site.

Yahoo! Search Marketing and Yahoo! Advertising

Overture (formerly Goto.com), the largest pay-per-click search engine, started its "pay for performance" listings in June 1998 and conducted more than one billion paid introductions a year for 80,000 advertisers at one time. Overture is now part of the Yahoo! Search Marketing program.

Yahoo! Sponsored Search is a form of search engine marketing that lets you create ads that appear in search results on Yahoo! and other sites in the Yahoo! distribution network.

Yahoo! allows you to test several versions of your ads and automatically displays the ads that receive the most clicks. You can also set specific start and end dates for your ads, and it offers a keyword generator to help you get ideas for building your ads. You can target prospects broadly or narrowly on a geographic basis and customize your ads to control costs.

Secret Tricks of Pay-per-Click Marketing Experts

People search the way they think, and the search terms that they use come from their own personal slang and culture. Too often, people designing the pay-per-click campaign for their Web site use their own slang, jargon, or corporate lingo. They assume that, because they refer to or think of things that way, it will be how other people search for things. However, this kind of thinking limits the number of Internet users who will see their advertising. Keep an open mind and think of all the possible words and terms that could be used to search for your services or listings.

While the first line of your ad is treated differently by different pay-per-click programs, putting your keywords in the title is usually a good idea. Use your prospects' words to catch their eye. Test different ad wordings, and you will find out what works best. If your ad's performance was particularly poor, however, you may not be allowed to bid on that phrase again. You need to be prepared to deal with the challenges you will face from your competition in today's competitive market.

"Free," "instant," and "bonus" are words that will get the attention of your visitors. Words like "call now," or "get yours here," persuade the reader to click on the link to your Web site. There are certain guidelines for each pay-per-click program, and you should read these carefully so you fully understand them. If you do make an error, you will be cautioned the first time, but after that you may be ignored. You must execute a plan ahead of time to make sure you are following the rules and your search terms are legal. The search engines have no regard for any issues that Webmasters may have and your campaign will suffer as a result.

List your domain name below the title to influence the reader's perception of your ad's quality and relevance. If your domain name sounds too promotional, you may consider getting a new domain with a more relevant-sounding name. Remember to think like a real estate buyer or seller. You may be the most conscientious and efficient real estate professional in your market area, but if that is what you put in your ad, forget a big "click-through ratio" (the percentage of searchers who click on the ad).

If I am a prospective buyer searching for a condo in Miami, Florida, and I search for the words "Miami condos for sale," I will be most likely to click on an ad that leads me to believe I will find a lot of Miami condo information on the site. "Miami Condo Specialist" is okay, but "All Miami Condo Listings Here" is more likely to get my click.

Use the search term in your ad copy. Studies have shown that using actual keywords or phrase in the ad copy will increase clicks. As in the example above, it reinforces the idea that I will find what I want to know about "Miami condos for sale" if the ad says just that. For example: "Find Miami condos for sale; maps and more here."

Take your visitors directly to the page that highlights the exact property or service you are advertising in your pay-per-click campaign. Do not take them to your home page. There should be a link to your home page from the property listing or service page. The keywords you use in your pay-per-click campaign should be targeted to the property listing or service page.

Pay-per-Click Marketing Tactics for Cheap

While Google and Yahoo! lead the pack when it comes to pay-per-click advertising, there are low-cost alternatives. Follow these guidelines when choosing low-cost PPC outlets to get the most out of your online advertising dollars:

- Compare PPC pricing models and offerings to find the best deals.

- If you have a limited budget, use do-it-yourself PPC outlets.

- If your time available is limited, enlist the help of a search engine marketing firm.

- Maintain your PPC budget by using localized pay-per-click advertising.

Some of the smaller PPC search engines are worth looking into. The most popular ones include Findwhat, Kanoodle, Enhance Interactive, and LookSmart. They will not get you the same exposure you may get with Yahoo! and Google™ AdWords, but you can still generate a respectable amount of traffic with them, and they are much less expensive.

Bid on common misspellings and variations of keywords to save money. For example, "cheap" could be changed to "low cost". Keyword research tools are offered by many of the bigger companies, and these help locate common alternates and misspellings of your keywords of interest so you can pay less for the same amount of traffic. There are more complicated keyword research tools available that let you see how much to bid to get a particular ranking (such as the number-one spot), before you finalize your bid. Some also provide traffic estimates so you can see how different keywords and phrases you want to bid on will perform.

There is a variety of autobid software you can use to do the bidding for you. The software program will track the items you are bidding on using different keywords. It will also adjust your bid to give you a high ranking so Web visitors can find you better. Autobid is one such software that is popular and offered by Yahoo! and Google as well as some of the other pay-per-click Web sites. There are bid management programs that will allow you to set a definitive bid price to match your budget so you meet your advertising goals without overspending. This will also stop you from bidding when you have reached your budget. This works in your favor when the bidder that is below you lowers their bid, because the bid management program will automatically lower your bid and keep your ranking while you pay less for it.

11

BANNER ADVERTISING

This chapter explains what a banner ad is and shows how to properly utilize it to get prospective real estate buyers or sellers to your Web site. It also spells out how to get other local businesses to put their ads on your Web site in exchange for advertising your business on their site.

WHAT ARE BANNER ADS?

Banner ads are an image with embedded HTML code that act as a hyperlink when launched. The HTML code tells the Web browser or server, to pull up a certain Web page when someone clicks on the hypertext displayed in the banner as text, graphics, or a combination of both. Generally, a third-tier server is utilized to track the impression and "click-through."

One of the most popular methods in the recent past to market a business online is through the use of banner ads on other Web sites. They are generally published through a centralized server, or they may be embedded directly in the Web pages. A feature of the embedded banner ads is that they can be rotated through a variety of scripting methods or from features within a Web design application, such as Microsoft FrontPage, so they do not have to look the same or say the same thing.

The most common way of paying for banner ads is a pay-per-click system. The number of clicks is tracked using software. Each click will generate revenue to the Webmaster hosting the banner ad (not the advertiser). Generally, this is less than $0.10 per click. The advertisers do not make any commission on the click through; instead, you may get a new real estate buyer or seller. These banner ads are similar to traditional roadside banners or billboard advertisements. They alert potential consumers of the product or service and strive to create enough interest to get them to click the banner and travel to your Web site and buy your products or services. The ads also allow you to be more dynamic when it comes to your advertising techniques because you can change the way the image looks at any time and you can add unique forms of animation to the banner ad. Banner ads are typically annoying, and many Internet users consider them as spam or a nuisance. Newer and more recent versions of Web browsers have the ability to block most pop-up banner ads.

There are several reasons online or brick-and-mortar businesses may choose to use banner ads to promote their products and services. Some of the reasons include:

- To drive more Web traffic to their Web site.

- To boost sales of their products and services.

- To alert their customers to any special deals they are offering or any new listings or services they have.

- To publicize their name on the Internet so potential clients know who they are.

How Do Banner Ads Work?

More and more people are using the Internet each year to make money. This is an opportunity to participate in the boom of the Internet. Internet advertising techniques typically obtain good results. Advertising is one of the largest money makers on the Internet, and banner ads are one of the most successful methods of prosperous advertising. Banner ads are images that are programmed with a hyperlink so that the Web browser loads a certain Web page when someone clicks on the banner. Generally, a third-tier server is utilized to track the impression and "click." Usually, banner ads are an integral part of an effective affiliate program, which we will cover in Chapter 12. Overall, banner advertising success is on the downhill trend. Click-through rates have dropped steadily, and there has been much discussion about the untimely death of banner ads. It cannot be argued — banner ads are no longer the cash cow they used to be; however, they are still an effective, low-cost form of advertising, and many companies successfully use banner ads in their marketing and advertising portfolio.

Click-Through Rate (CTR). This is accepted as the definition of the measure of how effective a banner ad is. CTRs range from the industry average of about 0.35

percent to 10 percent. As a general rule, the more targeted the site, the higher the expected CTR. If set up this way, some banner ads will only be displayed when a particular keyword is entered, making them better targeted toward the person seeing it.

Branding is another important feature of banner advertising. Banner ads promote branding techniques, as potential customers become familiar with your "brand" and recognize it when displayed in banner advertisements. The idea is that potential customers will get familiar with seeing your business name and, when the time comes for them to buy or sell property in your local area, they will choose your real estate company over a competitor's because you are familiar to them.

DIFFERENT TYPES OF BANNER ADS

There are several types of banner ads to advertise your listings or services. You can choose to alter the shape and size of the banner ad to suit your purposes. There are eight standard sizes of banner ads, as indicated by the Internet Advertising Bureau (IAB). These banner ad sizes are based on a pixel, which is the unit, or section, of color that creates the images you see on your computer or on a television. The standard sizes for banners, as dictated by the IAB, are as follows:

- A full banner: 486 by 60 pixels

- A vertical navigation bar on a full banner: 392 by 72 pixels

- A half banner: 234 by 60 pixels

- A vertical banner: 120 by 240 pixels

- A square button banner: 125 by 125 pixels

- Button size, number 1: 120 by 90 pixels

- Button size, number 2: 120 by 60 pixels

- A small, or micro-size, button: 88 by 31 pixels

The most frequently used banner size is the full banner, at 486 by 60 pixels. However, you will find all sizes of banner ads in all areas of the Internet, with many variations on the standard sizes. You do not have to use the above banner sizes, but they are the most common, and you should stick to the standards whenever possible. Banner size is also dictated by the amount of memory size that can be given to the banner. The majority of Web sites limit memory from 12K to 16K. Banner ads will add to the total size of the Web page, and therefore many Web sites limit the amount of memory allotted to banner ads and other forms of Internet advertising. The more memory a Web site takes up, the longer it will take to load on the Internet, and you want your Web site to load fast and correctly. This requirement will put a limitation on the size of the banner ads you use on your own site and the ones you place on others' Web sites.

When you look at the existing banner ads on the Internet, you will notice there are many different varieties of graphics and animation. Some of the most simplistic banner ads will have only one JPEG or GIF image on them that links the banner ad to the main Web site of the company doing the advertising. By far, the most popular of all the banner ads is an animated ad that uses a GIF animation tool. GIF animation allows the banner ad to change over a few minutes, showing various GIF images one after the other, and many times in a flowing sequence. These ads instantly grab the attention of visitors to the Internet and are sure to make people notice your banner ad. There are many programs available that help you create animated GIF images; a good one is included with Corel's Paint Shop Pro (**www.corel. com**).

Another type of banner ad uses media rich tools, such as Shockwave programming, Java programming and audio, and video techniques. This type of banner ad adds to the Web site memory size since it needs larger files to support the rich media programming. These tend to make up the bulk of the annoying, nuisance-type banner ads; in addition they are more expensive to create. Animated GIF ads are simpler to create on your own.

Reasons for Using Banner Ads

You have decided to use banner ads for advertising your Web site and business and you want to entice visitors to click the ad so they go directly to your Web page. The visitor to your Web site would not have arrived at your site if it were not for the banner ad they saw. Essentially, this means the person may have been searching for property to buy in your area or for a real estate agent to list a property for them, so you need to keep that in mind when designing the banner ad. Each ad may or may not generate a new client or sale from the banner ad click. Statistics show that banner ads amount to a measurable percentage of Internet sales, even though that number is on the decline.

If you are going to host ads on your Web site, there is no cost for doing so, and you will get paid for the click throughs generated, regardless of whether they result in a sale or not. A low-bandwidth banner ad on your site is a good idea. If you wish to use banner ads as an advertising campaign, there are many services that offer banner ad hosting, exchanges, and marketing. Banner ads are also effective when used in conjunction with an affiliate program, which we will discuss in the next chapter.

A question you need to answer is: How do you measure the success of your banner ad? There are several ways you can measure how successful your banner ads are to know if you need to do something to change them:

- **Measure the amount of page views.** Page views are also known as "page impressions." Page views are calculated by how many times a particular Web site is requested to be seen from the server. You will not be able to measure the success of your branding techniques or how many sales you have achieved through the banner ad, but you will be able to determine how many people are reaching your Web site by clicking on your banner ads. Most space for banner ads is sold according to the cost of one thousand page views, or impressions, you receive.

This is also known as "cost per thousand."

- **Measure the amount of clicks.** This is the number of times Web surfers click on your banner ad. Many Web sites will sell banner ads according to the cost per click (CPC).

- **Measure the amount of click throughs.** This information about your banner ad indicates the ratio between clicks to page views, or click-through rate (CTR). This ratio measures the number of people who have arrived at your Web site by clicking on a banner ad. The number of people who find your Web site may be less than 1 percent, but this 1 percent is just as important to the success of your Web site as the other 99 percent.

- **Measure the cost-per-sale.** The cost-per-sale will indicate the amount of money you spend on banner advertising to make a sale of your listing or to get a new client to list a property with you. You can use what are known as Internet cookies to keep track of the amount of traffic to your Web site from banner ads. All of this information is important in helping you determine how to effectively use your banner ads and what is an appropriate budget to dedicate to this type of advertising.

How to Make Banner Ads

You have decided to create a banner ad. You can give several reasons why it is a good investment and you have chosen the style of banner ad that best suits your needs. Now it is time to make one, but how do you go about making your own banner ad? With minimal knowledge about computers, you will still be able to make a simple banner ad for your Web site. Making a banner ad is simply a matter of coding and imaging with HTML hyperlink tags that link back to your Web site. You will be able to develop the graphics for your banner ad with the use of graphics software programs such as Paint Shop Pro or Microsoft Digital Image Suite. The following is the simple coding that is used for a banner ad:

```
<a href="http://www.YourWebSiteHere.com"> <img src="http://static.YourWebSiteHere.com/gif/banner-ad-static.gif"> </a>
```

You can make simple banner ads on your own without too much computer knowledge, and GIF-animated banner ads are not much more difficult to make yourself than any other banner ads. If you want to use banner ads filled with media, such as Shockwave programming, Java programming or audio, or video techniques, you may want to hire someone to do the banner coding for you; however, this is typically not cost-effective for an emerging online business.

You want your banner ads to look as professional as possible so you can keep up with your competition. If you want your banner ads to stand out in the crowd, you may want to hire a professional designer. You want to hire a professional who is able to create a banner ad that promotes your real estate services or listings and quickly grabs the attention of Web visitors so they want to click on your banner ad. The price you pay for your professionally designed banner ad can vary from as low as $75 to as much as $1,200, depending on what type of banner ad you want and how much you are willing to spend from your business budget for advertising with banners. A well-kept secret is a Web site called RentACoder, where you can post projects for thousands of computer programmers and designers to see, and they bid on your project. You will find programmers in the developing world who will do small projects like these for next to nothing, since the U.S. dollar is worth a lot in their country.

You can find Web sites that will allow you to create your own banners for free. You will be able to combine different banner sizes with font, color, and images to create the banner you want for your advertising purposes. If you are wondering why these Web sites offer this type of service, the answer is easy:

1. They want to post their own banner on your Web site.

2. They make a certain amount of money from the advertising that is located on their own Web sites.

3. Banner creation is their own hobby, and they want to share and use the banners as a personal reference or in their portfolio.

Some free banner creation sites that you can use include:

- Atomic Arts — **members.tripod.com/atomicarts**

- Make Your Banner — **makeyourbanner.com**

- ABC Banners — **www.abcbanners.com/mlinks/ links.pl**

The type of banner ad you develop can be as simple as you like or as elaborate as possible. The choice is yours when it comes to how much time and money you are willing to allocate from your business budget for banner ads.

Successful Banner Ads

In our quest to design a successful banner ad, we must keep flexibility in mind. There are no strict guidelines you need to follow when creating and designing your banner ads. Success is achieved in different banner ads for different reasons, and it is up to you to find out what works for you and your business and what you need to change. You may have to try a few different types of ads for a while and track how well they do before making changes and modifications, until you find the perfect type of banner ad for you. There are no hard and fast rules as to what works in Internet advertising and what does not work. However, there are some things you should know about banner ads so you stand a fighting chance when it comes to effectively designing your first ad.

One important rule for success is to place your ads on Web pages that have content with a relationship to real estate, such as home inspectors, mortgage Web sites, or home improvement sites. If you are promoting your real estate business, your banner ads may not be too successful if they appear on Web sites focused on how the real estate market nationwide has crashed. Internet advertising studies show the more relationship there is between banner ads and the Web sites on which they appear, the greater the number of clicks that take place. If you are creating your banner ads yourself, make sure that each ad promotes a particular listing or service that you offer and does not merely promote your Web site. Emphasize your ability to sell a property, or the properties you have for sale, not your Web site.

When Web visitors see a banner ad advertising a Web site, they are less likely to click and find out more than if the banner advertises a certain product or service that they are interested in. Every banner ad should be a reflection of the things you can do for the client and not about your Web site alone. Banner ads should take Web visitors directly to the portion of your Web site where that listing or information about your service is located. You do not want banner ads to link to your home page, since this means visitors will have to read your site to find the listing or service they clicked to see. Banner ads are designed to get you the sale, not to find potential clients who have time to browse your Web site.

A wise choice is to place your banners at the top of the Web page. If you put it further down the page, it will be hardly noticed. Visitors to your Web page browse the page quickly and you have to try to get their attention. The banner ad should be in a location that will catch the visitor's eyes immediately.

You should focus directly on making your banner ad simple and easy to grasp. The more complex you make your banner ad, the less likely you will interest your visitors to click on the ad. You should get your visitors' attention fixed on your ad and they should be able to understand the message you are trying to send. A popular form of banner ad display is animated banner ads that stand out on a Web site. This will guarantee more click throughs for you. Be sure to design your banner ad to the property or service you are offering. Do not let visitors be confused and wonder if they have arrived at the correct Web site once they click through. They will lose interest and leave your Web site, and you may lose a valuable prospect. Your advertisement needs to be clear and concise.

Do not get too technical with your banners so that your page takes a long time to load. Your Web visitors will move on to the next Web page. Also, other Web sites will not put your banner on their site if your banner is too big. If your banner is a reasonable size, the Web pages it is on will load much faster. Banners that are large tend to drive your Web visitors away. Their looming effect presents a feeling of intimidation and is an absolute turn off to any visitor who comes to a Web page. The banner ad needs to reflect the theme of the Web site so the visitor will feel at home, and will stay longer and be comfortable enough to trust the information that they receive from your Web page. You can experiment with different types of designs and themes until you are confident they will meet your Web visitor's approval. The Internet is an ever-changing advertising medium, so you have to keep abreast of these changes. Your Web visitors are the perfect candidates for giving you any feedback you need to help you consistently keep your Web site updated to match the changing trends of the Internet.

A banner ad is essentially a means of developing the right target audience, so you must create a banner ad geared toward a certain group of individuals who want to buy or sell a property in your local area. Your market research or existing knowledge should provide you with the relevant information about your target audience: what they like, how they shop, what motivates them to click on certain ads, and how you can get them to your Web site. This targeting technique is important to successful Internet marketing. An experiment with pay-per-click ads will give you some of the information you need. You will be able to discover what makes the target audience click on your pay-per-click ad according to how you word your pay-per-click ad as mentioned in the previous chapter. Armed with this information, you can create your banner ad with some of the same words you used in your pay-per-click ad headline. Therefore, your pay-per-click keywords can prove to be valuable when making a banner ad.

Advertising and Banners

In taking the necessary steps to implement banner ads for advertising your product or service, there are options that can simplify the process for you. There are three basic options from which you can choose:

- Purchase ads on certain Web sites that will be the

hosts for your banner ads.

- Create or use an existing a banner exchange program, where you post the banner ads for other advertisers, and they post your banner ads on their Web sites.

- Pay a fee to join what is called a "banner network," where you can post your banner ads on a certain number of host sites according to the amount of money that you have paid. An example of a successful "banner network" is Double Click (**www.doubleclick.com/us**).

Decide which options are best for you and your business. You may want to choose the exchange program option if you do not have the budget to pay for posting your banner ads on other Web sites. If you decide to exchange banner ads, there are two methods you can use. The first is to establish working relationships with advertisers on other Web sites so you can exchange your banner ads and host them on your sites.

Using this method, you will be able to put your banner ads on Web sites that closely match your own or where you know potential customers may see your banner ads and be interested enough to link back to your Web pages. The only disadvantage to this method is that you need to spend a lot of time looking for banner exchange partners for you to have a significant number of banner ads on the Internet.

The second method of getting your banner ads online is to use what are called "banner exchange programs." You will become part of a huge network of Internet advertisers that each host a variety of banner ads on their Web sites, whether or not there is a similarity between the Web sites or any relevant content on the site. Banner exchange programs are explained further in the next section. No matter what method you choose to use, when it comes to getting your banner ads on the Internet, you will be giving your Web site and business the cutting edge you need to stay on top of your competition.

How to Buy Advertising

One way you can increase the effectiveness of your banner ads is by buying advertising space on the Internet. There are several ways you can buy advertising:

- Join an affiliate program.

- Join a banner exchange program.

- Contact Web sites on your own to buy advertising space.

- Hire an agency that specializes in Internet advertising.

You will find that there are advantages and disadvantages to using each of the above methods for buying advertising.

Use an Affiliate Program

Pooling resources using affiliate programs is an effective

way to place your banner ads on other Web sites as well as to save you time and money. You can join other affiliate programs, or you can start your own affiliate program that will enable you to pay the sites that are hosting your banner ads only when there are results to show for the click of your ad, or when you sell a property to a customer that found your listing by clicking on the banner ad. The nice thing about using affiliate programs is that you will not have to buy a large number of page views or click throughs. Instead, you will be paying only a certain amount of the profits that you generate from obtaining a new customer, which amounts to a minor percentage of your overall profits. We will discuss affiliate programs at great length in the next chapter of this book.

It is possible to start an exchange program as explained previously in this chapter. A banner exchange program is a great way to get your banner ads on many other Web sites. When you use an exchange program, you will not have to do the legwork and contact other Web sites about hosting your banner ads. Essentially, a banner exchange program is a system of brokers, where the program acts on your behalf to place your banner ads on appropriate Web sites on the Internet. A network of banner ad programs is much the same as a banner exchange program, but there is one drawback to using a banner ad network: You are giving up most of the final decision-making power about where your banner ads are going to be placed, as well as what banner ads you will be hosting on your own Web site.

Spend the time and effort to make sure you look around before choosing a banner exchange program or network. Some of the larger banner networks will sell great advertising space on some quality, highly trafficked Web sites; however, you may find the fee for advertising on these high-traffic sites is too high for your advertising budget. One thing you should be looking for when it comes to using a banner network are those programs that will sell what they call "an excess of banner locations." These are simply banner spaces they have not been able to sell at the regular price and now need to get rid of at a discounted price.

Another decision you have to make if you are choosing to use a banner exchange program is whether you want to use click throughs or page views (impressions) when determining the success of your banner ads. You will find that banner ad networks will deal with one or the other method of tracking the number of hits to your banner ads.

Some large banner networks that measure banner ads by page views (impressions) include:

- **www.burstmedia.com**

- **www.ContentZone.com**

- **www.doubleclick.com**

A couple of large banner networks that measure banner ads by the click-through method include:

- **www.eads.com**

- **www.BannerSpace.com**

CONTACT WEB SITES ON YOUR OWN

Personally seek out Web sites and approach their owners on your own to see if they will place your banner ads on their Web pages. Although this can take up a lot of your valuable time, it has several benefits you may be able to take advantage of. One of the biggest advantages is that you will be in charge of the final decisions about on which types of Internet Web sites you place your banner ads. You will be able to determine what Web sites will most benefit and relate to the products and services you are selling. You will have the ability to target Web sites that do not have a lot of other banner ads on them so your banner ads become more effective.

Being selective about where you place your banner ads can result in a big payoff when you target the sites that have a certain appeal to the same people who are interested in your products. You will have to do your research before you contact the Web sites where you want to place your banner ads to make sure the site is what you are looking for. Many Web sites will have certain processes in place that you need to follow before you can place your banner ads on their Web pages. You first need to see if the Web site has Web pages that have room for any type of advertising. If you are unsure about whether the Web site will accept banner ads, the only way to find out is to contact them using e-mail. You should take your time choosing the right Web sites to target so you do not waste your time contacting sites that do not fit into your banner ad campaign.

Many of the larger Web sites that accept banner ads will have some type of a package available for Internet advertising. This advertising package may come at a high cost that will quickly eat up your advertising budget. Most of these large Web sites will use the CPM (cost per thousand) method of tracking page views, or page impressions, which means you will be paying anywhere from $10 to $125 for each thousand page views you receive from your banner ads. Web sites that have a high traffic volume will charge more than less-traveled Web sites, so you should do your research before you make a final decision about which Web sites you want to place your banner ads on. Usually, you will be buying bulk packages of page views (impressions) at one time. Some typical page view packages are anywhere from 50,000 page views to 200,000 page views. A good thing to keep in mind is that many smaller Web sites that have less traffic will not have advertising packages available for you to place banner ads. This often means that you can make special deals with the smaller Web sites that will be mutually beneficial.

HIRE AN AGENCY THAT SPECIALIZES IN INTERNET ADVERTISING

The ultimate method of buying advertising is to hire an agency that has a great deal of expertise in advertising on the Internet. If you hire an advertising agency that offers all the available services, you will have little to do when it comes to your banner ads. These advertising agencies will help you to find the best Web sites to place your banner ads on and will find the best price for your advertising budget. You can also hire an agency that will help you create your banner ads as well as manage all of the advertising for your online or brick-and-mortar business. Many times, you will find large advertising agencies are able to get a more competitive price than if you were looking for Web sites yourself on which to place your banner ads. This is because agencies are able to buy page views (impressions) in large quantities.

While there are many advantages when it comes to using advertising agencies, there are some disadvantages you need to consider before making your final decision about whether or not to use an agency. One of the most significant disadvantages is that many advertising agencies will not deal with small Web sites that are looking for help with their banner advertising. Each advertising agency will have different services that they offer, and this may include what is called an "account minimum." If you have a small Web site as well as a small advertising budget, you may not find an advertising agency that is going to start an account with you and your Web site.

Look around before making your final decision about which advertising agency you want to use to help you with your banner ads and other advertising needs. The questions to which you want to find answers before making your choice are as follows:

- How much experience does the agency have?

- What are the rate costs associated with the different services the advertising agency offers?

- What services do they offer?

- Are customer referrals or client testimonials available?

In the long run, it may be worthwhile for you to hire an advertising agency since they will be able to give you the knowledge you need to keep up with your competitors and their banner ads. Even if you are a smaller company with a smaller Web site to promote, you may want to consider hiring an agency so you gain the Web presence you need on the Internet to reach your customers and potential customers. Internet advertising can be tricky if you do not understand all the elements that go into successful advertising. You want to have as much of an advantage as you can when it comes to getting your company name out there so you can increase your profits as well as your customer database. You can use Rent A Coder (**www.rentacoder.com**) or Craigslist to find more affordable individuals to provide the same service as the advertising agencies for a fraction of the cost.

How to Sell Advertising

After you establish your Web site on the Internet, you not only can buy advertising, you can also sell it. When you sell space on your Web site, you will be able to receive some revenue that you can turn around and put back into your own Web site or business. However, selling banner ad space on your own Web site can be a bit tricky.

One of the simplest ways for you to sell advertising on your Web site is to become part of a banner ad network so you do not have to be in charge of the advertising you have on your site. The banner network will allow you to keep track of the amount of money you earn from selling advertising space, as well as take charge of the banner ads that are placed on your Web site. The only thing you need to keep in mind if you are using a banner ad program to sell Web space for advertising is that it will take a certain percentage of the profits made from selling this advertising. There will always be more Web sites selling space for advertising than there will be Web sites interested in buying the space. It is for this reason alone that banner ad programs will be a bit particular about the advertisers that they list.

You will find most of the banner ad networks have monthly Web site traffic minimums that they require to participate in banner ad programs. For instance, there are some banner ad networks that set a minimum of at least 250,000 Web site visitors before you can join their banner network. Some other banner ad networks have a set of tiers that determine how much you pay based on the amount of traffic that hits your Web site each month. A tier system works well for smaller Web sites so you can choose a banner ad program that your advertising budget can handle. If you have a Web site that gets a large amount of traffic each month, such as more than 90,000 page views (or impressions), you will have no problem joining a banner ad network that uses this CPM method of calculating Web site traffic. However, if your Web site generates less Web traffic each month, you will need to look at banner ad programs that calculate Web traffic using the click-through method. Do not forget though, that using the click-through method of Web traffic calculation means that you will not be making much money on the banner ads you host on your Web site. This is because you will not be paid until a Web visitor clicks on the banner ad and links to the Web site that is being advertised. The average click rate is less than 1 percent, so your revenue from the click-through method will not amount to much at the end of the month.

THE PROFIT OF HOSTING BANNER ADS

You will probably not make a fortune selling banner advertising space on the Internet, but you will still be able to collect revenue that you can turn around and put back into your advertising budget. Most of the banner ad networks on the Internet have what is called a "run of site" type of ad that they sell to businesses advertising on the Web. For each of these ads, they are getting approximately $4 to $5 per page view, or page impression (CPM). From this total, the banner ad program will deduct anywhere from 30 to 50 percent as its share of the earnings. This leaves you with about 0.2 to 0.3 cents on each page impression that occurs on from Web site. You need to have about 100,000 page views, or impressions, to earn $250 to $300 for any given month.

When you join a banner ad network program, you usually will have little say about the type of banner ads that are placed on your Web site. This means that visitors to your business Web site will be seeing ads that may have nothing to do with real estate or your local area, and in some cases, you may feel the banner ads are having a negative effect on your Web site. If this is the case, you can sell your own advertising space and be choosier about the type of banner ads that appear on your Web site.

If you are going to be selling your own Web advertising space, you need to be aware that there are many other Web sites selling advertising space as well. This means you need to have a Web site that stands out from the rest and on which advertisers want to see their banner ads. Many advertisers are looking for Web sites that have a certain type of content and a high volume of traffic each day. This is because quality Web sites receive more page views, and this means a higher chance of Web site visitors clicking on banner ads hosted on those Web sites. When you are looking for advertisers to place their banner ads on your Web site, you need to influence them to decide that putting their ads on your Web page is going to be good for their business.

First you need to provide potential advertisers with statistics about your Web site such as information about the type of visitors your Web site receives and what your traffic volume is per day and per month. Then, you need to demonstrate to them that your own products and services are relevant to the business they are promoting. Next, you need to make sure you have the technology available and in place to host banner ads if you are going to be selling advertising space on your own. You need to be able to host the banner ads as well as keep track of the number of visitors to your Web site as accurately as possible so you are able to charge the advertisers on your Web site accordingly. Selling your advertising space will be more time consuming than if you joined a banner ad network program and let them do the work for you. However, if you want to have the Web site for your business grow in the direction you want to take it, you may want to invest the time and effort it takes to sell your own advertising so that you get the look and feel to your Web site that you want.

12

Affiliate Programs

This chapter will describe how to get businesses to become "affiliates" of yours, so they can promote your listings or services on their Web sites. When a site visitor clicks on one of your listings or ads, they are taken back to your Web site to complete the transaction. The use of this affiliate program is tracked by a click-through method and the affiliate is given credit for the sale. Generally, affiliates earn 8 to 15 percent of the total sale for doing nothing more than allowing your listings or ads to be shown on their Web site. It may be more appropriate for you to pay a commission to the affiliates for these sales leads, rather than using the typical commissions based only on sales. One of the largest successful affiliate programs on the Internet is through Amazon.com, which has more than 600,000 affiliate Web sites in place at this time. If you want to expand your online business, your goal is to have others become affiliates of your Web site, just like Amazon.com does.

Generate Leads by Offering Cash Incentives

For most cases, the arrangement between affiliate Web sites is based on the total number of Web visitors they send to your site, the number and total dollar value of sales that you get from the people sent to your site, or the number of clicks you get from their site going through to your site. When you use affiliates to send Web visitors to your site, you are taking advantage of a marketing technique that is extremely effective, while at the same time, very affordable for even the smallest business Web site owners.

There are three separate entities involved with each of the actions that take place when creating and successfully implementing an affiliate program:

1. The Web site of the affiliate,

2. Your business Web site, and

3. The Web visitor or customer, who you are trying to attract to your Web site.

Often, there is a middle service, which is an affiliate tracking application or server that records the click-through transaction.

Who Uses Affiliate Programs?

You may be wondering just what type of Web sites and businesses use an affiliate program. Most businesses lose out and miss valuable opportunities at increasing their business potential by not adding affiliate programs for their Web site. Most Internet business owners would do well to add an affiliate program as an option for their visitors. Any product or service marketed on the Internet is a candidate for an affiliate program even if it is a big-ticket item. As long as you are selling something on your Web site, you can incorporate an affiliate program as part of your sales package. Many Web sites use an affiliate program to make more money than they make selling their own products by themselves.

If you do not want to include an affiliate program on your Web site, you may consider adding more income to your Web site business by advertising someone else's affiliate program on your Web site. Make sure it is similar or it complements your real estate business before you engage in any affiliate program. Most Internet marketers are seeing the value of affiliate programs and getting involved whether it is with a small Web site or a big advertiser. Advertisers have different modes of calculation to assess how much they should pay their affiliates.

Affiliate managers employ three commonly used methods to pay the affiliates who participate in their program:

1. **The pay-per-click method.** This is the most popular method. The affiliate manager sets up a special link for each affiliate and the affiliate is compensated each time a Web visitor clicks on the special ad link. This works out to be a numbers game. The more clicks affiliates get, the more money they will make. It is not mandatory for Web visitors to buy

anything when they click the affiliate link. As long as the affiliate can get them to click the link, money is being made for the affiliate. The trick that most successful affiliates use is to create an eye-catching and thought-provoking ad headline that will get the Web visitor to click the link to learn more. Of course, once they click and are forwarded on to one of your Web pages, your content needs to be catchy to convert them into a buyer or seller.

2. **The pay-per-lead method.** This type of payment method will allow you to pay your affiliates each time the visitors they send to your Web site input their contact information into your lead generation form. If your affiliates get visitors to the contact form on your Web site and instruct them on how to fill out the form, you will pay them.

When you acquire the contact information for several new prospective buyers or sellers, you can follow-up with them to try to make a sale or get a new listing. But, you do not have to make the sale initially. A good way of not scaring prospective clients off is to offer useful information first to establish yourself as a reputable agent or broker. Once you effectively use your auto-responder to keep in touch with these potential clients, and even give them a phone call periodically, you will get the sale eventually if you are a persuasive salesperson. Your affiliates will have done their job by getting the visitors to leave the appropriate information you need to make the sale. You can build your client base from the information you receive.

Make sure your pay per lead expense is less than the future business you are able to secure. This can be a more exact way of setting up your Web site's affiliate program, but it will be far more costly per lead than it is per click. That should not be a problem once you are converting a percentage of these leads into clients.

3. **The pay-per-sale method.** This method allows you to make money from the actual sale of a property. This is a lot more complicated to accomplish than the last two methods, but that does not mean it is not possible or useful. Because this is complicated, few real estate agents, if any, use this method of affiliate marketing, which will set your Web site apart from the competition in terms of gaining quality affiliates that want to make lots of money promoting your listings.

   The payment agreement you make with your affiliates makes money for them each time they send a visitor to your Web site who buys a property you have listed. This is a good incentive for your affiliate to send more targeted traffic to get a sale each time they can send someone to your Web site. The key is to decide on a way that both you and your affiliates agree on to track where your buyers originally came from. Finding a way that uses a third-party affiliate system is even nicer because your affiliates do not have to worry that you may be dishonest by not letting them know that the visitor they sent to look at your listing purchased the property several weeks later.

As with the other two affiliate methods, your Web site sales copy should give the visitor exactly what the affiliate promised in their advertising. You can get someone to write good Web copy for you to engage your audience and get them to look at your listed properties. This method requires for you decide in advance what percentage of the commission or a flat amount you will be paying your affiliates per listing they get a buyer for. An example of this type of affiliate program can be found at Amazon.com. They only pay their affiliates when the affiliate sends a customer and that customer makes a purchase.

If you are not going through an affiliate company, you will have to work out the details of your affiliate program yourself. You should make a decision whether you will pay your affiliates monthly or weekly. A monthly payment plan is what most affiliate managers use. There are two methods of affiliate payment that have been added to enhance the world of affiliate programming. These are residual payment programs and two-tier payment programs.

The residual payment program is one that will entice any affiliate member because of the high-income potential available. Affiliates are able to make long-term income as long as the Web visitor they send to your Web site continues to purchase the same product or service. In most cases, this works well with membership subscription sites. Affiliates who become a part of this program will remain with you for a long time and will send you a lot of visitors so you both can make ongoing income. You may think this is not applicable since you are selling real estate and not something like make-up or vitamins, which a customer will buy monthly or every few months. While you are correct in thinking that, it is time to start thinking outside the box. Earlier in the book, we touched on the concept of sending out a newsletter. If your newsletters contain valuable enough information that you have a huge database of satisfied subscribers, you may want to consider charging a modest subscription fee to your newsletter. This will allow you to utilize the residual affiliate model described above.

The two-tier payment program is another concept for which you have to think outside the box, since it allows affiliates to have a structure similar to network marketing organizations such as Amway or Avon, and allows each affiliate to profit through commission sales and sales recruitment. In addition to receiving commissions based on sales, clicks, or leads stemming from their sites, affiliates in these programs also receive a commission based on the activity of affiliate sites they refer to the merchant site. Though this is definitely not a common affiliate marketing model for real estate, it is not an impossible one to use.

You may also, on occasion, run across some affiliate payment agreements that use the page view, or "pay-per-page-view" (impression), payment method. With this method, you will be paying your affiliates a total that is determined by the number of Web visitors who look at your banner ad. This type of payment agreement is just an advertising technique that is linked to them putting your banner ads on their Web sites, as revealed in the previous chapter. There is one big difference between an affiliate program and an advertising program such as banner ad network programs: In an affiliate program, you only pay your affiliates when the action, such as a sale, a click, or a page view, is completed.

HOW AFFILIATE PROGRAMS WORK

Affiliate programs work quite easily once they are correctly set up; however, there are many processes that run in the background and that are necessary for the smooth operation of these programs. You will need to have someone — yourself or someone you hire — keep a log of the actions that determine how your affiliates are paid. This means keeping track of the number of sales you generate from your affiliates and the number of page views that occur after Web visitors have visited your business site via your affiliate's site. Most reputable affiliate software packages automate this task and simplify the process by keeping track of all affiliate sales, affiliate earnings, affiliate payments, and other critical information. Here are some of the items that need to be tracked:

- **Web Visitors.** the total number of Web visitors who arrive at your business site after clicking on your link on your affiliate's Web site.

- **Banner Ad Browsers.** The total number of Web visitors who notice your banner ad on your affiliate's Web site.

- **Affiliate Generated Leads.** The total number of Web visitors who enter their contact information while visiting your business site after clicking on your link on your affiliate's Web site.

- **Sales.** The total number of Web visitors who generate

an actual sale after arriving at your Web site via your affiliate.

To maximize your effectiveness, you need to keep accurate numbers on the above actions so your affiliates are paid accordingly. Even though it may seem to be a lot of effort and time for you to closely administer your affiliate program by yourself, you will find that the advantages outweigh the disadvantages. When you have complete control over your affiliate program, you will be able to decide with which affiliates it is most beneficial for you to work.

Affiliate Program Networks

If you have never been a highly organized person or you are busy selling houses, as you should be, and you want to avoid all the administrative work you can, you can join what are called affiliate program networks, or "affiliate brokers." Affiliate networks act as the go-between for you and your affiliates. These network programs keep track of all the activity that occurs on your Web site and your affiliates' Web sites that has to do with the payment agreement you set up. Affiliate networks take care of all the payment agreements and methods, keep a log of all the actions that take place between your Web site and the affiliates' Web sites, manage and maintain all of the links and banner ads that need to be set up on your affiliates' Web sites, and keep your affiliate program in a list of available affiliate merchants within their network directory. An alternative to affiliate program networks is purchasing a stand-alone affiliate program, which you install on your Web server, such as ProTrack (**www.affiliatesoftware.net**).

A benefit of using an affiliate program network is that you

will have access to a number of different types of affiliate programs at one time so you can mix and match your payment agreements. This way, you can "test drive" several programs at once, without the hassle of setting them up yourself, so you will be able to find the best kind of affiliate program that works for you and your business. This can save you a lot of time and effort which is one of the many advantages of using an affiliate site. You have to pay a commission fee when you join an affiliate program network. Usually, the cost of using an affiliate network is about 15 to 25 percent of each transaction that occurs. This is worth it since it saves you the time of doing it yourself.

There are many affiliate companies that can serve as the liaison between you and the affiliates marketing your listings. A good example of one such affiliate marketing company is ShopXML. They currently have about 5 merchants selling their products through about 1800 affiliates' Web sites. This system works great for the traditional pay-per-sale model, but has not yet been altered for the nontraditional real estate transaction model. That is not to say that ShopXML or similar affiliate companies would not be interested in figuring out the details of getting this set up for you. Talk to a few of these companies and you may find one that could set up a successful pay-per-sale affiliate system for you.

Becoming Part of an Affiliate Program

With all the benefits of affiliate program networks, you should seriously consider joining one, when you consider that joining is a way that you can have a lot of people marketing your listings online while you focus on other aspects of your business. Before you take part in an affiliate program, you need to decide what role you want to play in the process: the affiliate, the merchant Web site that affiliates, or a combination of both. We already provided all the reasons you will most likely want to have affiliates who will send potential clients to your site and increase the success and profits of your real estate business. But since you also have a portion of your Web site that offers content rather than listings for sale, you may want to be an affiliate for a few business Web sites as well. Appropriate products to list on your site for an affiliate commission are books about how to buy and sell real estate, or anything related to moving in or out of a property.

The bottom line is that you need to decide how your Web site will best benefit, and take the steps to becoming an affiliate, having some affiliates, or being a little of both.

There are several steps required that you need to take to be an affiliate for other Web sites. They are easy to implement. All you need to do is find an affiliate program network site on the Internet and join by filling out a simple application form that gathers the following information:

1. Personal information, such as your name, address, and the type of payment plan you prefer, including payment address.

2. Information about your Web site, such as your Web address (URL), the name of your Web site, and a description of your Web site.

Once you have filled out the information form, you will be asked to sign what is called a "service agreement" so both you and the affiliate network are clear about the terms and conditions.

It may be necessary for you to wait a few days to find out if your application has been approved, at which time you can choose the type of affiliate programs that appeals to you the most, and in which you would like to take part (most merchants have only one option in terms of pay-per-click, pay-per-lead or pay-per-sale). After you have chosen a few affiliate programs, it will be time for the "merchants" to view your Web site to see if they want to use you as an affiliate.

Once you have been approved, the affiliate program network will help you in hosting the links and banner ads on your Web site that correspond with your chosen merchant's products. At this time, you may be asked to work out the finer details of the payment, such as which action you are going to be paid for and how much, such as pay-per-click, pay-per-lead, or pay-per-sale. However, this is typically set in advance. Most affiliate programs will only pay you once a certain minimum amount of earnings has been reached because the profit you make as an affiliate is not usually thousands of dollars, since it accrues a few cents at a time. This is so the affiliate network does not have to send out small amounts of money that cost more to send than you made. Additionally, most affiliates do not honor sales for purchases you make through your own affiliate link. After you have been set up as an affiliate and understand which actions you are being paid for and how much, you can concentrate on the content and purpose of your Web site.

To increase the amount of visitors on your Web site, you want to get affiliates to advertise you. You can either start your own affiliate program, and have complete control of your program, or you can join one of the many affiliate program networks. Joining an affiliate network will save a lot of effort on your part, as you get help starting the affiliate program, and the network chooses your affiliates and does the work for you.

Getting Started in the Affiliate Network

Joining an affiliate network usually starts by filling out an application form where you answer some questions about your Web site and what products or services it sells. You will also sign a license agreement with the conditions and terms of the affiliate program. To become a member of the network, you have to make some deposits and pay a fee. Most networks will charge a one-time fee when you join and a yearly fee as well. Depending on how successful the network is, joining it can cost from $500 to $6,000. Other expenses, such as paying your own affiliates and a portion of each payout to the network, will also raise the cost of the program.

An advantage to joining a network is that an advertising budget is created that includes the entire cost of the setup of the affiliate program. A good affiliate network should also provide detailed information about everything that happens in your affiliate program, such as payments to your affiliates, and distribution of the banner and links to your Web site.

It is possible to choose your own affiliates with most affiliate networks, since they often make it available for you to choose any Web site interested in linking to your Web site. This option is becoming common because people want more control over their affiliate program. By joining an affiliate program network, you will not have to do all the hard work yourself, because it is done by the network. If you do everything yourself, you will have to find the right affiliates, buy software to keep track of affiliate actions for correct payment, distribute the banner and links to your Web site, and be available at all times to answer any questions your affiliates may have. Should you decide to run the program yourself, you can either buy software that keeps track of the actions of your affiliate's Web sites (such software will cost from $150 to $600), or you can join a Web site that will keep track of the affiliate actions and sell the information to you.

How Affiliates Link to Your Web Site

After you have established your membership in an affiliate network, the next thing you need to know about how an affiliate program works is how your affiliates are going to link back to your business Web site. There are several ways this can be accomplished, depending on which method works best for you and your Web site. Here is a list of some of the more common methods of having your affiliates link to your Web site:

- **Banner ad links.** Banner ads use a combination of text and graphics to catch the attention of Web visitors so they click on the link and end up on your Web site.

- **Text and content links.** Text links on your affiliate Web site are mixed in with the content of each Web page and usually appear as blue text so Web visitors can click on the text and link to your Web site. Text links are a great form of advertising because they are less intrusive to the eye of a Web visitor than other advertisements that many Web visitors are trying to avoid. Using text links in the content of Web pages is becoming more popular as advertisers search for ways to make advertising on the Internet more subtle.

- **Co-branding.** With this method, your affiliates can have their own separate identities on the Internet, while, at the same time, have visitors to their Web sites link to your business Web site unknowingly. Your Web site will handle all of the sales for your business, but you will appear on your affiliates' Web site, so Web visitors often will not know they have been on two different Web sites. This is probably not a good option for your real estate business, because you want to establish your business name as the best one in your local area to all prospective clients who see your Web site. This type of affiliate link or arrangement defeats the purpose of all the branding you have been working so hard to establish.

Why are affiliate programs a successful and profitable choice? The main reason is that when you use an affiliate program, you have the ability to use links to encourage people to visit your Web site, browse your content, browse through your listings and services, and potentially become clients in your database. By using an affiliate program, you are advertising your Web site and listings through hundreds or thousands of other Web sites throughout the world, dramatically increasing the exposure and potential sales for your profits at little or no cost.

For the most part, affiliate programs work best when the affiliates, the merchant, and the links have something in common with the product or service being sold. When you, as a real estate agent or broker, make wise choices about which affiliates you want to host your Web links, you have a better chance of catching the interest of clients and potential clients. You come out ahead because you get those clients you may not otherwise get with only your online marketing efforts, while at the same time, your affiliates come out ahead because they can be linked to real estate listings, which presumably have something to do with their Web site, without ever having to be a real estate agent or broker. If you are using an affiliate network program, the network also comes out ahead because they earn a profit by bringing you and your affiliates together and taking care of the finer details of managing the affiliate program for you.

13

BLOGGING

This chapter describes a relatively new fad in online journaling — blogging — and shows how it can get you recognition as an expert real estate agent or broker in your area. It explains the details of what to blog about to get potential clients to your Web site. The topics that should be stressed in creating a blog are the agent or broker's knowledge of the particular locality, and the process of purchasing or selling property. A blog should make a personal connection with a client or potential client by offering insights into the community and suggesting the agent is more knowledgeable than the average agent.

Since there has recently been a dramatic increase in how many agents are competing for attention and business on the Internet, it is important to create a presence that is different from everyone else's. Social and relationship marketing have made blogging an important tool to consider if you want to stay ahead of the game. Internet marketing has been evolving in so many new directions due to the rapid advancements in technology, and blogging is the relatively new fad that is getting rave reviews.

Blogging is a perfect match for real estate agents and brokers, especially since many already spend their day answering questions, commenting, and helping many people to make the life-changing decision to buy or sell their homes. It takes time for a real estate agent to develop a relationship with a client, but with a real estate blog, agents will be able to transform how the public views them on an individual basis. Since real estate is a knowledge-oriented type of business and the Internet has become a search tool for a lot of real estate enthusiasts, without a doubt, real estate blogging is a reliable means of attracting more clientele and making more information available to those prospective clients.

It is a crucial time in the real estate market today, so real estate agents have to use creative ways to market and to acquire good leads. Before you start your blog, make sure you identify your audience and implement the blog according to that specification. Look at other real estate blogs online to get an idea of how you do and do not want to build your blog.

Blogs give agents an outlet for cost-effective — if not free — advertising and a way to inform their clients and romance their new prospects to a place of loyalty and trust. Without a blog, you would be missing out on the secret success of blogging that the competition has been hiding, the means of establishing yourself as an authority in your field, and a platform to get your message to an information-hungry audience.

Internet marketing can become expensive with pay-per-click ads, banner ads, and other forms of advertising previously explained. However, blog marketing is one of the most innovative and cost-effective ways that real estate agents are using to capitalize on the market today. It is one of those secrets the other agents wish we had not told you about.

If an agent uses the blogging environment to expose defects, and inadequacies in a home on the market, this will create a sense of trust and honesty for buyers, though it may create resentment from the listing agent or seller, so be careful what you blog about.

Blogs can be used in many more effective ways than traditional marketing can. Blogging has turned the real estate landscape into a formidable tool for any agent who is bold enough to transition into something so exceptional.

Real estate professionals are now starting to catch the wave of this new market because it reaches more people and sells more homes. Blogging creates a window of opportunity that may not have been possible with other offline methods of advertising. It creates a sense of community, trust, and interest. If done the right way, blogging can be an extremely successful medium of marketing online.

Since most buyers and sellers search for information about real estate online, it would be beneficial for any agent or broker to own a team or individual blog to reach these buyers and sellers. There are more than 70 million people who are blogging online already, according to Technorati, and it has been estimated that as of 2007, 31 percent of Americans on the Internet are reading blogs. Most agents do not realize that this is an untapped audience with a huge potential for increasing their bottom line. This is the perfect opening to getting new leads and lasting friendships.

The traditional way of real estate marketing is still a great way to develop relationships with clients, but the real estate blog marketing is more definitive and saves time. The opportunity to add real estate blog marketing to your advertising portfolio is a productive way to initiate your Internet presence and carve out a niche for your market.

Real estate agents are realizing that the Internet is the place where most of their prospects congregate. If they are not making their presence known on the Internet, they are missing out on a ripe crowd of buyers and sellers.

Blogging requires an investment of time, but every agent knows how important it is to be prepared at all times to deal with the changing real estate market. Real estate blogging will be worth your time in the long run, especially in this current competitive and challenging market.

How Blogs Enhance Your Image

Make sure you choose a unique domain for your blog page. You can use a free blog site, but if you want to look professional, it is better to buy your own domain name. You already know how to buy your own domain name based on the explanation in Chapter 2. Look for a suitable domain name for your blog the same way you did for your main business Web site. A few examples of good domain names for a blog are HoustonPropertyInfo.com, BuyingHousesTruths. com, RealEstateSecrets.com, and BuyingChicagoCondos.

com. Search for keywords like property, houses, real estate, blog, and the name of your town or city. Conversely, you can buy the domain name for your blog that is your existing domain name with the word blog on the end, such as MiamiCondosBlog.com. Use an attention-grabbing headline and domain name to get Web visitors interested in reading your blog. Once you set up your blog and make it unique to your personality, you will eventually get some visitors who will identify with the message you are trying to get across to them. They will get to know more about you and become familiar with your expertise.

The real trick of having an effective real estate blog is to write only about a niche market. For example, if you know the most about commercial property in New York City, your blog should be focused on that and that only. Of course, if you know a lot about several niche markets in your area, it is absolutely acceptable for you to have several blogs, each on a specific niche market. For example, it is acceptable for you to have a blog about the condo market in Los Angeles, single-family homes in Los Angeles, and real estate investing in Los Angeles. The information you provide on your blog will portray you as an expert in your field and will grab the attention of targeted audiences.

If you can develop and define a strategy of providing information to your audience by writing search engine optimized, keyword-rich articles that confirm your expertise and give the prospective client information they were searching for, you will gain a captive audience that will either bookmark your Web site for future use, or pick up the phone to call you for help.

Free Resources for Your Blog

Choosing a blogging platform is easy. You can start with the free ones like Blogger (owned by Google), WordPress, and TypePad. You should get your domain name for your blog and redirect it to the free blog platform of your choice the same way that was previously explained for your main Web site.

The only problem with free blog platforms is that most of them do not provide much technical support, so you are on your own. Do not forget that anything can happen, such as Google can fail to save the page or have a page error without any warning, so it would be best to save all your blogs before uploading them to the actual blog site.

If you are technically inclined, WordPress has a lot of technical features to create a more interesting design. Blogology.org also has a wide supply of tools to make blogging an easy task.

Did you know you could use RSS feeds on your blogs? An RSS feed is a program that formats content for subscription. This means anyone can subscribe to your feed and get all the fresh content you provide from your blog. With RSS feeds, anyone interested in the information you are blogging about can get an update with your new blog posts each time you add a new one. And it can also be a promotional tool since it sends messages to subscribers automatically.

The Web site at **www.rsspieces.com** offers a lot of free ideas, resources, and tips that will assist you in building your blog and making it interesting.

Other ideas for enhancing your blog are to get or write a downloadable eBook on a real estate topic of your choice and offer it as a free gift to your visitors. If you have a main site, be sure to link your blog to your main site. Share your wisdom by offering a free tip of the day. Keep everything simple.

Exchanging links with other bloggers or Web sites helps to make your blog visible. Choose other blog sites that relate to your theme. Search engines will rank you higher depending on how many links are directed at your Web site.

KEEP YOUR BLOG SITE FRESH

Podcasting has become quite popular. This is the concept of attaching audio or video recordings to your blog posts so your audience can download it to their iPod and listen or watch your message while on the go. This gets a lot of attention and it gives your blog a more visual presentation of what you intend for your audience to learn. You may also do an interview with a reputable person in the community and show it on your podcast. Though this is a more advanced technique, you may want to try it once you have a regular dedicated audience reading your blog posts daily.

The future of real estate blog marketing is giving clients an opportunity to subscribe to the blog by supplying their contact information. This allows the Realtor to get more new clients through the process called "pull or permission marketing." This is a powerful way to introduce yourself and develop a long-term relationship with potential clients.

Writing articles and contributing daily informative posts will help to keep your blog fresh and delightful to read. Try to use fewer articles written by other individuals. Your customers need to know what you have to say. Make your articles personal. Put humor into it. In your articles, highlight your knowledge by giving information that will benefit readers. Use specific keywords in your article that will enable people to find, thereby from search engines and increase your traffic.

The best way for a busy Realtor to blog is to post a few sentences or paragraphs every day about one topic. You can write about whatever you dealt with on that day, an idea you had for selling a client's property, a deal you are putting together, or even a "day in the life of you." Whatever you post, make it focused and with a point. Even if it is about your bad day, make sure there is a moral to the story, like "Even on a bad day I still had five potential buyers look at this new listing."

Let your audience see your vulnerability by remaining true to who you are and allowing them to see you are a real person. Make your blog post show your personality. Post at least two times per week even when you are extremely busy, since any less than this leaves your site with "stale" posts. If your audience comes back to your Web site and finds you missing in action, they will leave and not come back. You want to make them feel important, special, and that you would go to any lengths to provide good content just for them.

Invite your visitors to make comments on your blog so you can get to know them and make sure you answer any questions they may put in their comments. This will show you are interested in what they have to say and want to continue to nurture the relationship you have established.

Include a link from your blog posts to an online virtual tour of any of your real estate listings that you mention in your posts. This will allow the reader to see the details of the properties you are talking about, creating interest in potential buyers. Instead of driving from their location to see a home they may not end up buying, buyers can save time by looking at the house from the comfort of their homes based on the interest you sparked with your blog post.

Use your blog for giving the latest real estate news and trends. You want to become the one-stop convenient location for information. This can be as simple as the monthly trends in your local area, national real estate trends, or insights into where you see the market going. You will be able to increase brand awareness, stimulate the demand for more information, and create a competitive advantage in your field of expertise.

Include a newsletter subscription as an option to your visitors. Let them know you are serious about providing ongoing information to them. They will be impressed by your commitment.

Fresh content is the most important aspect of maintaining a successful real estate blog. If you cannot create fresh content at any point in time, get permission to use someone else's content so there are still regular posts being added. That being said, you should maintain fresh content, written by you, whenever possible.

Blogging is the easiest way to get indexed in the search engines because of the fresh content it provides. Search engines love fresh content and will index your blog if you continue to provide fresh content.

Here are some creative ideas that you can use to enhance your blog:

- Highlight a celebrity home for sale, and make it newsworthy. People are curious about celebrities and will flock to your blog site. If there are no celebrity homes in your area, cover a story about a high-priced home in the area.

- Build a list of important things needed when selling a home. People love tips.

- Mention any new construction or major development projects in the area.

- Talk about the current market conditions and a projected turn of events if you have an educated guess on the subject, or if another expert has provided information you can use. People are curious to know what is going to happen in the future.

- Explore any local resources that deserve mentioning like new facilities, parks, libraries, and recreational centers that exist or are planned, but not yet constructed.

- Provide a review of a fine restaurant, nightclub, or school in the area.

- Provide a little harmless gossip that is buzzing in the community.

- Provide a report of why sellers should make sure their open house is successful. Sellers will feel led to read the entire blog post.

- Create a checklist for the home buyer — especially for the first-time home buyer — on what is needed to purchase their home.

- Blog about different types of mortgages and mortgage lending.

- Highlight a foreclosure sale. People are always looking for a bargain and it will create an interest.

- Create a video of the alternative traffic routes in your area so readers can learn a new way to avoid bad traffic.

- Inform your customers about the crime rate in the community.

- Most people want to know about the history of the community. Discuss the history and highlight key areas of interest.

- Discuss details on how to prepare for any natural disasters that are relevant to your area, such as hurricanes, floods, tornadoes, or earthquakes.

Plan or map out the scope of your content. It has to make sense to your audience. Think about what you want to divulge. This should be identified before you start your blog. You do not want a blog that is not in line with your theme or is not organized. Decide how often you will be publishing an article or post. Determine what your categories are going to be. This will give you more focus. Make sure each blog post is separate and has its own link. The search engine picks up each link and displays it separately, so you can attract more visitors to your blog from the separate links you provide.

Keep Your Blog Marketing Focused

You can dominate your market by effectively utilizing your blog and by staying focused on your customers. List your blog in all the blog directories that focus on real estate or business of any kind. Use your blog articles as a stepping-stone by submitting them to article directories to get more exposure.

Use your blog to post community information, tips on the home-buying process, tips on the home selling process, and other real estate services you may offer.

When you continue to make regular posts to your real estate blog, in time, your name will become prominent on the search engines, and you will become a well-respected real estate marketer among your peers. This will reinforce that you are an expert in your industry.

Make your blog interactive so you know what your customers' needs are. Start a thread or comment that invites a reaction from your audience and the information you gain will help you create a more focused marketing strategy. This can be a place to perform a little focus group word-of-mouth research by creating a blog post about it and asking the audience what they would tell an acquaintance about you.

You can also create a guide on how to sell a home after a divorce. This is considered a niche market. Some people do not know what to do after a divorce, and your expertise would be a welcome relief to them. This will usually get new sellers interested in listing their property with you since they think you have experience helping divorced couples sell their houses.

Use comparison marketing. Show people what the market price in a certain community looks like and what your local area has to offer.

Include your blog URL on your business card and other marketing materials so that your prospects are aware you have a blog as part of your Web presence.

Blogging not only helps the Realtor, it empowers the buyers and the sellers reading the blog since it allows them to make better choices and find an agent they are comfortable with. Using the information gathered from a blog and from the established relationship with the Realtor, a seller, or buyer puts you at an advantage during the transaction, and may even help you to get a better price.

When you start your blog for the first time, you will feel isolated because it will seem as if you are writing for yourself. Do not get discouraged because in no time, your blog will be on the map for everyone to see and hear your voice. When that time comes, be sure you are writing for your target audience. Do not deviate from your niche market. If your blog is about you as a condo expert, there is no need to blog about the single-family home market in your area.

Develop the purpose and goal of your blog. This will help you focus on how you want to proceed and how you are going to maintain your real estate blog.

Blog About Past Successes

Mention some of your past experiences and success in your blog. This is referred to as "example marketing." Relate to a problem or problems you have solved in the past. People will learn that you are a problem solver and that you can do the job. They want to know you are qualified to sell their home or can help them to buy a home. This is the perfect way to establish yourself as an expert in your field. People will identify with examples of your experience and problems and want to hear about how you solved them. Some ideas and examples are:

- How I helped a home owner save his or her home from foreclosure.

- How I got a home buyer into a home for $20,000 less.

- How we closed in less than 30 days.

- How I got the appraiser to lower his or her fee for the home buyer.

- How I simultaneously helped a homeowner to move into his or her new home, and sold his or her old home.

As mentioned before, people want to know personal things about you. This is human nature. Without getting too detailed, provide a glimpse into who you are and why you have been so successful. You do not have to do it in one post. Over time, your audience will find out more about you as you mention more about your personal life.

Inform your audience why you decided to become a Realtor, what the obstacles are, and the successes that got you to the point you are at, and what your short-term goals for the future are.

More Ways to Make Your Real Estate Blog Successful

Your real estate blog site should come across to your audience as being a place not only to come for information, but also somewhere to hang out. They will see that you love what you do. It is your job to develop and improve your skills as well as have a good rapport with your audience. Prospective clients will feel more comfortable opening up to you and sharing information with you that will help you to further assist them. Be creative in implementing ways that they can feel secure and important all the time, and they will share your real estate blog space with you.

Be positive. Your audience will be able to tell what is going on with you, so be sure to remain upbeat. Acknowledge when you are having a bad day. They will empathize with you and possibly identify with you as well. They will know you are a real person and not one searching for a commission check. They will think their friendship is more important to you than a sale.

Collect the names and contact information of anyone who comments or contacts you through your blog. You should probably do this manually at first, but you will be able to automate the process later on. This is important in marketing in general, not just in your blog. For your blog and your offline business, you never want to forget the name of a prospective client. If you are sending an e-mail, making a comment, or making a phone call, be sure to identify the person by his or her name. It will make the individual feel like he or she has a personal relationship with you.

Real estate blogging will eventually create word-of-mouth advertising for you when readers find out how you treat your prospects and customers. As your blog grows, so will your audience. Be enthusiastic about your blog. Your visitors will feel your vibe. Do not over-design your blog; this is the one mistake most bloggers make. Stick with a basic warm color and forget about any fluff. Be believable and direct. All this will make your blog simple but interesting — just what your audience wants.

Successful blogging will depend on your commitment and consistency in providing exclusive information that will educate, amuse, and empower your audience.

14

UNLOCKING THE SECRETS OF EBAY

This chapter reveals the hot new real estate market on eBay, how to best tap into it to sell listings, and how to attract local and national buyers.

HOW TO ADVERTISE REAL ESTATE ON EBAY

Millions of people today use eBay as a means to auction off all sorts of items. Many individuals refurbish items and sell them on eBay for a tidy profit. There are a lot of people who use eBay as a steady form of income. Some people have even started setting up an eBay drop-off storefront. How about using eBay to draw in potential customers in the vast world of real estate?

Newspaper articles, online classifieds, and other forms of advertisement are usually site-specific, found only by typing in keywords pertaining to that area if found online, and by being in a certain location for newspaper classifieds.

Not only does eBay have higher traffic than any other method of listing a house, but it is not specific to a certain location, and is accessible from any location at any time. The real estate market thrives on buyers who purchase multiple properties and own land across the United States. Most of these people have an independent business of their own, and keep track of their assets as the real estate market rises and falls. They make renovations to properties they have purchased, and sell for a tidy profit when it becomes a "seller's market" in that area. You can see why a national, high-traffic system like eBay would be beneficial to the world of real estate.

The real secret here is that, on any given day, if you do a search in the real estate section of eBay for the keywords Realtor, agent, broker, MLS, or other keywords indicative of an agent-listed property, you will not find any agent-listed properties. Buyers have fewer qualms about buying a property listed through a Realtor than they do about buying from the owner. This is because they think the owner may try to rip them off, whereas they think that, if a Realtor is involved in the transaction, it is more legitimate since the Realtor has a career and reputation at stake. Since there are so few Realtors using eBay, this is an open market for you because you will get more potential buyers interested when they see a Realtor has listed the property. Of course, few Realtors use eBay since they need the seller's permission to use this unusual way of listing and marketing their property. But never assume sellers will not agree. With today's slow real estate market in certain areas of the country, there are a lot of sellers eager to try new methods of selling their property.

The first step in listing property on eBay is to obtain a screen name, and build a seller profile that has good ratings. This may be a little difficult if you have not used eBay in the past, and do not have any previous transactions through the site. Two options around this are using a friend's eBay name who has good ratings, or selling a few things on eBay beforehand to get some positive feedback. It is recommended that you use your own profile since you want to use it to market your main Web site and your other listings. When choosing a screen name, try to get the same name as your main Web site. For example, your screen name may be HamptonsVacationHomes if your Web site is HamptonsVacationHomes.com.

Obtaining positive feedback on your new profile is as simple as completing a few sales, selling some personal items you want to get rid of, and making sure you hold up your end of the bargain. In other words, you need to ship the item out on time, make sure the item is packaged properly, and give the buyer positive feedback when the transaction is done.

The next step in listing a piece of property on eBay is to decide what type of listing you would like to run. There are two different ways to list property on eBay, and you can find the rules and regulations on the site about this particular type of listing.

1. **Auction/Fixed-price format.** You list the property as a regular auctioned item, but the price you put down (the "starting bid") is your asking price. A buyer can "bid" on the house and make an offer

through the listing, as well as get your information to negotiate a price on a more personal level, via e-mail or whatever information you decide to keep in your user profile.

2. **Classified ad**

   You post the house listing and all the information as you would on any other online classified Web site or newspaper, and all users have access to your property details through the eBay search engine.

With each of these types of listings, you can see who has accessed your eBay page and who is watching (getting updates through e-mail or profile notices) your "bid" so you can be proactive and contact the users to provide them with further details on the property.

Once you have chosen the type of listing that you want, and have successfully posted the property on eBay, you may get overwhelmed with the amount of enquiries you receive from curious users. Take the time to e-mail back and forth, and answer questions that may be flooding your in-box. Do not be afraid to be choosey with whom you decide to communicate; after all, you might be meeting a few of them in person.

BENEFITS OF AN EBAY STOREFRONT

Another type of storefront getting popular in the world of technology is the online eBay store. This online business opportunity is geared toward the heavyweights of eBay. High-volume sellers can set up their own eBay stores (powered by eBay itself), and sell large quantities of one item or similar items independently.

All the information needed to get a start with this business opportunity is on the eBay site. Sellers have the option of listing items that can run for months at a time, instead of having to repost, which makes organizing and managing one of these hot new markets much easier. Often, eBay searches will return these stores as a search result if the store specializes in that particular item, which means even higher traffic, and in turn, more profit.

The virtual eBay store has many more advantages if you have several listings at a time; included in your store's site is a listing of all the other regular eBay items you have listed for auction at the time. Anyone who looks at one of your listings and goes onto look at your store will see all of your listings, as well as a link to your main Web site.

Be aware that eBay requests a small monthly fee to keep your online storefront up and running, but chances are if you have gotten to the point that you are considering having an eBay store, the fee will seem like nothing compared to the commission you are making each time you sell a listing through eBay.

Listing and selling property on your online eBay store is just as easy, if not easier than listing a regular item auction. With your online store, you will have all of the organizational help provided by eBay to keep track of your property listings, potential buyers, and running times.

GENERATING MASSIVE LEADS USING EBAY

Once you have your listings up on either independent auctions or through your new eBay store, you can use eBay to network with a multitude of potential buyers who visit your site or that you show the properties to. There will be a lot of people looking at your listing and contacting you for more information about the property, or to see the property in person.

As the real estate agent, you will up your sales substantially by diligently keeping a file of interested buyers in a specific area to show other properties to. Buyers who may have "bid" on your listings in the past and were keeping a watch on your pages, or who e-mailed you to get more information on a certain house you were selling, should all be contacted when you have similar properties listed that you can sell them.

Make notes and keep an organized record of who is interested in what type of house and in which areas. The next time you get a listing to sell a comparable property, you can go through your file and call up the potential buyers to see if they are still seeking something similar.

Always include the same information on your eBay page or online store that would be on your business card so people have multiple ways of contacting you. Also, try posting a picture of yourself by your contact information. A customer might be more inclined to trust you enough to meet you in person if they know what to expect before setting up an appointment.

In the world of real estate, eBay can be as profitable a tool as you let it be. Remember, always give feedback; you will get it in return, and your eBay sales will continue to grow and grow.

15

Hiring Help for Less

Outsourcing projects to individuals who have the skill to perform and complete tasks in less time than you is beneficial to you and will free up your time. Do not be afraid to delegate a variety of skilled or unskilled tasks. Try to hire help who will give you good quality work, but for less, to stay under budget.

You can outsource any task while you spend time building your business, attending meetings, and servicing your clients. The good thing about hiring help is that distance is no longer an issue. With the use of e-mail and the Internet, hiring a skilled individuals to work out of their homes has become popular these days, and is not uncommon among business owners.

These individuals work at a remote location, and are able to set their own personal daytime hours. They are usually unsupervised unless you want certain deadlines to be met. You will not have to consider any office expenses for these individuals because they should already have their own computer, software, Internet connection, and telephone. The only thing that is of concern to you is that they are professional and will get the job done, and that you have the money to pay for this expense.

Today, business owners are finding that there are many more choices available for hiring help for less and getting the support they need to get more done.

HIRE PROJECT-BY-PROJECT

You could consider hiring individuals who are talented and experienced in skills such as Web page design, SEO, creating auto-responders, blog or forum postings, writing articles, and designing an eBay store. This can be done on a project-by-project basis. There are several Web sites dedicated to helping you find freelancers to do your projects. On some of these Web sites, individuals bid on your project over a set period of time, depending on how much time you have to find someone to do it.

If you are looking for a Web designer, you may ask questions about what type of e-commerce site they have designed before. It would also be good to know if their skills are beginning, intermediate, or advanced. In other words, how much HTML or other programming languages do they know?

After the bidding ends, you choose the individual you think matches your requirements. Most of the time, you will be able to see the individual's portfolio posted, and be able to assess their skills. If you are considering someone to write articles for you, you could ask that individual to write a test article to see their writing style, after which you would assign the tasks that you would like to be completed. Make sure you give the individual a deadline or set time of completion. You are looking for someone who knows how to meet deadlines.

You should always have the person sign an independent contractor agreement and a copyright agreement. This will protect both parties. The copyright agreement will allow you to retain exclusive rights to any articles or information created on your behalf.

Payment should be agreed upon before you begin any project with the contractor you are hiring. Decide also how often payment will be sent and in what form. Some may have a PayPal account, which enables you to send money via the Internet; however, you need your own PayPal account to use this method. If you are paying the individual after each project is completed, let them know. Otherwise, it would be best to work out a weekly or monthly fee to allow you to keep better track of these expenses for your accounting purposes.

HIRING STUDENTS AND TALENTS OVERSEAS

Many Internet marketers are utilizing students and talents overseas. Overseas talent often have a lower cost of living in their country, and students accept a lower fee than most skilled workers in the United States. You can find these individuals hanging out in some familiar locations like Craigslist, Rent A Coder, GetAFreelancer.com (**www.**

getafreelancer.com), Guru.com (**www.guru.com**), and Elance (**www.elance.com**). This is only to name a few. Hiring talent overseas can be a difficult process since there is a difference in time zones. However, it can be done, and will save you more money than hiring someone locally.

The best way to select a student is to put a small ad in a college newspaper. This is usually a cheap methods of advertising to find good help. Most students need to find a job to cover their college expenses, and will also work at a discount. You can find students whose major is computer programming, and they are often good Web designers. You can find journalism students who love to write, and have the skills to craft great articles and press releases for you. There are many talented students overseas as well, and most are articulate and skillful in a variety of tasks. Sometimes, the only challenge you may have is the language barrier, so it is recommended that you look for someone who speaks — or at least types — good English. Make sure you get a written sample to determine his or her skill in writing English.

On most freelance Web sites, the persons interested in working for you will be able to bid on your project. Most good candidates will have some type of portfolio and samples of their work that you will be able to look at. You can set your bid price range and the individuals will bid based on what they would like to receive for the project. You can decline any bid over your budget. Most of the freelance websites give you the opportunity to list your projects for free.

On the Get A Freelancer Web site and most of the others mentioned above, you will find cheap help. Most of these individuals live overseas and your project price can be set for a lot lower.

On Craigslist, you have to be very careful, because this is an open forum and classifieds Web site, so there is no profile or ranking of the individuals responding to your posts. However, you can find good help there as well. Craigslist divides the Web site into categories to make it easier for you to find what you are looking for. If you need a writer, you will be able to go directly to that category. You are also able to place your own ad to find a person with the needed skills. You can include all the details in the ad or set an auto-responder to handle the onslaught of e-mails that you may receive. Ask for a resumé in your advertisement so you will be able to peruse through them to pick out the ones that meet your guidelines.

THE BENEFITS OF A VIRTUAL ASSISTANT

This book presents enough ideas to make online marketing your full-time job, so it may be wise to utilize a virtual assistant to get these things done quickly and effectively, while you are still listing and selling houses (see VA corner on **epowernews.com**). What is a virtual assistant? These are individuals who can provide administrative, data entry, marketing, and telephone customer service skills.

If you want one virtual assistant to do all your tasks,TeamDoubleClick.com makes the process easier for you by conducting the interview to save you time. This company was created to provide virtual assistants for business owners who are busy and cannot find the time to look for someone. The interview process is rigorous for the virtual assistant and the decision to hire the individual is based on how they answer the interview questions compared to what the client is looking for. It takes up to a week or two for the best person to be selected.

There are also virtual assistants who provide telemarketing and cold-calling services. To protect yourself when using a virtual assistant for this purpose, you should have the virtual assistant sign a non-competetition/non-disclosure agreement before any work begins. Make sure the contract includes all your terms and conditions so if the virtual assistant chooses to walk away from the business relationship legally they cannot use your contact list for themselves or another real estate agent or broker.

All virtual assistants in America legally require a social security number, EIN or W9, and a signed independent contractor agreement. The individual or individuals would be responsible for their own taxes, medical insurance, FICA, and expenses.

Find out how many hours the individual will be able to work, and make sure you come to an agreement on whether the person will be able to work weekends or holidays when necessary.

Plan a telephone interview with the candidate to find out more information that e-mail may not cover. Before the interview process, you can let the person fill out a short survey to prepare you for the interview. One specific Web site you can use is **www.humanmetrics.com/cgi-win/ JTypes2.asp.**

To simplify the interview process, there are certain things you have to use to guide you in selecting the right person. Make sure you ask questions that will help you to hone in on the individual's skills so you can get to know the person more.

Look at the individual's work history to see how long they have been on different jobs. Make sure you compare the answers to what you want to accomplish with the assignment. Find out whether they are familiar with any technical terms that are used in the real estate business. Ask individuals about previous samples of their work, and if you are looking for Web designers, ask for the URLs to Web sites that they have designed. Get these samples before the interview, so you can have a better idea of what questions you should ask.

You need to ask for estimates if you are not familiar with the particular industry rates. Find out if the individual is comfortable with the assignment and if they have any questions. Find out what is the best way the individual will be able to be reached. Get an alternative phone number, if possible. Agree on a clear and concise communication medium. It will get rid of any confusion when it is time to get in touch because some people prefer e-mail and others prefer telephone calls. Make sure you have the individual do a small test project before you have them take on a larger project.

There are many online and offline businesses that have had great success with virtual assistants and have created long-term relationships that are still working for them. All you need to find the right person or persons is a careful interview and selection.

Here are some of the questions you should ask:

- What are your skills?

- On a scale of 1 to 10, how would you rate your skills?

- Do you have a problem working on weekends?

- How organized are you?

- On a scale of 1 to 10, how organized are you?

- What support system do you have in place?

- What are your hobbies?

- Are you comfortable with handling cold calls?

- If you saw a way the client would benefit from additional services, how would you handle it?

- If the client wanted to deal exclusively with you, what would you tell the client?

- How well do you follow up?

- Do you follow up with a phone call or e-mail or both?

- What are your strengths?

- What are your weaknesses?

- Why did you leave your last job?

- What did you like about your last assignment or last job?

- What did you not like about your last assignment or last job?

- Do you have a full-time job?

- Do you work for any other clients?

- If so, what type of business do they have? (You want to find out if this competes with your business.)

- How long would it take for you to finish an assignment?

- Is a 24-hour deadline something you would be comfortable with?

- What type of computer software do you have?

- On a scale from 1 to 10, how proficient are you?

- Have you taken any classes to improve your skills?

- If no, would you be willing to do so?

- If yes, what classes have you taken?

Be sure to pay close attention to e-mail and phone responses for professionalism and confidence. Ask for references from the individual. Get a phone number as well as an e-mail address for at least two references. It is wise to get the phone number and e-mail address of someone who the individual has worked with as a virtual assistant.

Know What You Want Done

Evaluate exactly what you need help with, especially the most technical and time consuming tasks that someone else can complete.

Make sure you write down what tasks you need to outsource. Whenever you are hiring a virtual assistant, Web designer, or writer, you will be more satisfied with the results of the work they do if you articulately describe exactly what you want done. If you put everything in writing, everyone will be clear on the responsibilities. Save these itemized tasks in a Microsoft Word document. You can post this document on the Web site where you placed your project description for bidding. This will prepare freelancers, and allow them to see what is being demanded before they place their bid. Sometimes your list of tasks will eliminate those who are not qualified to complete the work.

Clarify anything you think needs to be explained. Expound on any detailed description that may offer more information to the individual or individuals who are seeking to win your business.

Determine what your budget will be for each project, if possible. By researching industry rates, you can have an idea of what you have to spend. Virtual assistant rates range from $25 to $100 per hour. This can get pretty pricey if you have a lot of work, so you may want to find out how long it will take to complete your project, and set a definite price to be completed in a set amount of hours. It is then the virtual assistant's responsibility to finish the project in the allotted time.

You may want to ask the freelancers for a proposal and pick the one that meets your budget. It may not necessarily be the one who is more skilled for the job, so be careful when making your selection.

Start out with all freelancers on a project-by-project basis to see how everything works out. Try a small project first, and if the person proves himself or herself, you can add more assignments as you go along. Never assume anything about the freelancer or his or her work style. If you are uncertain about anything, be sure to ask the freelancer questions and give feedback. Always carefully look over any work submitted to you to determine if you want to continue the relationship or not. If you are unhappy with the work, you can give the person a second chance to make it right because you may not have properly articulated what you wanted. Do not be too quick to fire your hired help.

How Much to Invest in Getting Help

Freelancers are always searching for you. There are

numerous individuals on different freelance Web sites looking for legitimate jobs to do from home. The trend has become so popular that you will not have any problem finding someone. These are individuals who have worked in other organizations using the same skills that you are looking for. They will bring their experiences and skills to help you to get so much more done. Your decision is to create a financial plan to help you to get the most for your money.

You should calculate how much you are willing to spend on a particular project, based on the expected results. For example, if you are paying someone to run an AdWords campaign, how much money are you willing to spend to get 100 people to look at your Web site, assuming at least one will be a buyer or seller. With AdWords, you also have to consider the cost of the ad campaign.

You have to be able to find low-cost keywords to keep your budget down because AdWords can run your budget very high. Find someone who knows a great deal about AdWords campaigns, and let them give you a proposal on what it would cost you for the campaign and what their cost would be so you can determine if it is worth it or not.

Your expenses should not exceed your bottom line. You want to get the best results out of this experience. Therefore, going into the agreement, you will need to know what you are trying to accomplish and what it will take to reach your goals. If you are trying to get a paid client out of the project, you may want to find someone who has a track record in effective Internet marketing with a high success rate.

If you are using someone to produce blog or forum postings, you should have another individual create a program for you to track whether or not the individual who is doing the posting is working. You will be able to tell where a sale or client came from according to the HTML code placed in the posts. There are many companies that are using this technique to create more potential income.

You can hire both the individual posting in the forums or blogs and the person creating the HTML code from getfreelancer.com or any of the other Web site mentioned. Most of the bidders on these sites place low bids and can save you a lot of money and time.

Make sure you do not post an exact budget. Instead, post a price range, because a lot of freelancers will bid the exact budget that you post. If you post a price range, you will get bids that are a little lower than the highest range. If you want to have a logo created for your business, most any graphic designer would be able to accomplish this easy task as long as you explain your specifications. In that case, you would be wise to go with the person who has the lowest bid. However, if you need a Web site sales letter written for a specific audience, which is dependent on good copywriting, this is more complex and not everyone may have the skills to do exactly what you want. You may have to look for a copywriter who has particular experience writing for that target audience. You might not want to go with the lowest bid in this case; instead, choose the candidate that you have determined has the appropriate writing skills.

With all these dynamics to consider, you may be wondering how you will find a "diamond in the rough" to fulfill all the requirements that you are looking for. The answer is a long way from simple. The best advice is to follow the information in this chapter and use the tools on a freelance Web site, so you have a minimum risk of making a bad deal. Of course, if you are an attentive boss, you should not get ripped off or overcharged by your hired help, since you will know exactly what they are doing and when.

Conclusion

Now that you have completed this book, it is time to review and put these new techniques to use. In Chapter 1, the benefits of having several Web sites is explained, as well as ways to improve and utilize your existing Web page. Here are some ways to improve upon your Web pages:

- Control your links so they always link back to your site.

- Consider pay-per-click advertising as a means to draw in a larger amount of consumers.

- If you are linked to a large, nationally recognized company, link your main business page given by your company to your other Web sites.

- Include a photo of yourself on your Web site to make potential clients feel more comfortable about the possibility of meeting you in person.

- Become SEO savvy by recognizing the keywords a consumer would choose in their search for real estate, and use them in the content of your Web sites and listings.

Also explained in Chapter 1 are ways to go about attaining a new Web site, and optimizing Web pages in general:

- Make sure your site design is clean, professional, and informative.

- Consider using a professional Web site design company to build your new pages as their experience will give you a cleaner, more polished site.

- Remember to do your research on what is hot in the seller's world. (Do not forget to use your local library).

- Weigh the costs versus the benefits of optimizing your site.

In Chapter 2, we delve into the importance of a professional image, and ways to make advertising your business personal and unique. Here is a review of the main points and key tools to creating your branding:

- No one can promote you like you can promote yourself.

- Concentrate on your niche in the market and gear your campaign toward that.

- Create a tag line (short simple statement) and logo design to represent you.

- Work on a 30-second "blurb" that is a run-down of who you are and what you want to say to customers upon meeting with them.

- Many companies can help you design a logo that encompasses your brand.

The color scheme you use in your logo is important. Here is a list of colors and what they convey to the consumer:

White: refreshing, pure, light

Blue: serenity, loyalty, trust, wisdom

Green: natural, youthful, healthy, hopeful

Black: sophisticated, elegant

Red: uplifting, attention-grabbing

Do research by viewing other Realtors' Web sites, and take the time to look at the HTML coding so you can get a better idea of what keywords attract customers to the site. To do this, go to the tool bar, click "view," then "source" and the key words will pop up. Below are more examples of using keywords, as well as other ways of getting your Web site noticed:

- Use keywords in your domain name as well as your Web site.

- Creating a domain name is like creating a tag line; make it pertain to your potential clients.

- Consider paying extra to have multiple domain names lead to your Web site.

- Always include your Web site address in all business materials.

- Include on your Web site your real estate specialties, and any talents that you possess.

Chapter 3 covers media exposure and ways to get your business noticed. The following key points will help you get started by broadening your advertising methods:

- Consider using a variety of media, such as TV, radio shows, and press releases as a new way to introduce your business to the world.

- Contact your local newspaper to advertise by writing an editorial piece pertaining to your business.

- Cheap direct mailers are an inexpensive way to create many leads.

- Posting information about your business on your personal pages on sites such as MySpace, Facebook, LinkedIn, and hi5.

- Write an eBook that would appeal to either buyers or sellers.

The focus of Chapter 4 is on how to list your Web site in different sources. Directories work differently than Web sites. Rather than using keywords to draw in customers, directories use only your domain name or business name as a clickable link. There is a disadvantage in this respect because you are not in control of traffic flow. **Reals.com, Bestrealestatedirectory.com,** and **Realestateagencies. com** are a few of the main real estate directory Web sites. Here are the main reasons Web sites are rejected by directories:

- The administrator does not think your Web site has a professional look.

- Your Web site has no real content.

- You have submitted you Web site to the wrong category

To get listed in online phone book directories, go to **www. listyourself.com** to sign up, then call 411 to make sure your listing is being pulled up when requested. If your listing is hard to find, you can request that they make it more accessible.

Top search engines such as Google, MSN, Yahoo, and Ask, were explained in Chapter 5. We took an in-depth look on how they work, and how you and your business can benefit from understanding these Internet tools. Below is a list of search engine facts, and tips on using them to draw in leads:

- Search engines use automated software to send out "bots " and "spiders" to survey text on Web pages.

- Once you type in a keyword related to information found on these pages, the site will link your search to the results scouted from the "bots."

- Make your page new, pertinent, and appealing as well as rich in keywords to ensure optimum results from these search engines.

- Yahoo!® is a great source to find the most-used keywords pertaining to a certain subject.

- Using repeated keywords, to a small extent, on your page can increase the number of hits on your site. These repeated works obtain a higher ranking on search engine results.

- Keep keywords on your site at a minimum of 2 percent of the content so search engines will index the site.

- Consider blocking some pages on your site so "bots" cannot access and "crawl" them to expose confidential or irrelevant information.

- Rightmove and Zillow are two of the highest ranked property search engines.

- Buying keyword-rich domains and linking your site to other high-traffic sites can substantially increase your site's ranking.

Conclusion

Here are some tips on how to achieve higher rankings in search engines:

- If you have employees who have Web sites online, ask them if they would consider posting your Web site as a link on theirs.

- **Linkpartner.com** and **linkmanager.com** hook up people and their Web sites for linking to others.

- Research to see where your site appears in the search engines, and think of ideas to optimize your site to get a higher ranking.

- Consider sharing the load of this work with an assistant to help you attain high rankings and manage your Web sites effectively.

Chapter 6 explains detailed ways to optimize your site for maximum traffic and the highest rankings on search engines, as well as offering tips on designing your page. Here is an overview of the main points:

- Make sure your information is up-to-date, and consider paying someone to go through your Web site periodically to update it for you.

- Keep your message easy and simple.

- Limit the amount of graphics on your Web site.

- Do not use Microsoft Frontpage themes when creating a Web site since you do not want your layout to be the same as others.

- Be careful using frames in your site, as some of the content may not be visible to users with certain Internet settings.

- When designing your sales copy, keep in mind that another person will be reading it, not just a search engine.

- Pick a topic for each page and focus on this topic without straying.

Once your main keywords are decided, using them repeatedly is a strategy that will up the traffic on your site, as well as link more of your pages to search engine results. Advantages to this method and ways to implement are listed below:

- Different key words should be used on each page depending on the content.

- Think of what words you would use when searching for a property and use them throughout your site.

- Monitor your competitions' sites, and try to keep up with their methods for search engine optimization.

- Make sure your text contains the most important keywords.

- Do not use hidden or invisible texts in your page. Search engines know these tricks and they do not work.

In Chapter 7, there is in-depth information about the different types of Web site advertising, and the different Web pages you should consider making, as well as the advantages of using a professional Web page designer. Make Web pages for each of the following:

- Each listing, with a virtual tour

- Your blog

- Finding buyers looking for an agent

Web design mistakes to avoid:

- The main page does not quickly describe the focus of the Web site.

- Poor use or over-use of pop-up windows, catchy advertising, and splash pages.

- Letting your Web site be your only marketing campaign.

- Failure to make your Web site relevant with regularly updated content.

- Unnecessary text effects.

Advantages of using a professional Web page designer:

- If you have not been trained, it would be beneficial for you to hire someone who has.

- Use craigslist to find an affordable Web site designer

to accept a reasonable quote.

Chapter 8 guides the reader through the creation of a marketing list from potential clients who visit your Web site, and how to use permission e-mailing to gain addresses from potential clients without annoying or hassling them.

Other ways of capturing contact information include getting potential clients to sign up for free business newsletters, eBooks, and e-zines. Capturing potential clients' contact information, branching out into new advertising fields, and gaining a customer-friendly reputation can be done easily by utilizing these techniques:

- Include a subscription link in all major pages of your site for your newsletter.

- Offer special articles for your visitors to download, or write one of your own that pertains to an interesting topic about real estate.

- Put your e-mail address on the main page.

- Provide a "send to a friend" option in the sign-up form.

- Include links to your Web sites and newsletters in your e-mail signature lines.

- Put the link to your Web site and a short description on all printed material.

- Book public speaking engagements and seminars.

- Start a promotional campaign with a rented e-mail list.

- Promote yourself in articles.

- Include newsletter subscriptions in lead generation forums.

- Include opt-in information on satisfaction surveys.

- Convey trustworthiness.

- Create an e-zine with tips and information on homes and home buying with links to your Web site for advertising at no cost to you.

- Honor unsubscribe requests, and take users off your e-mail lists in a timely manner.

How to use an auto-responder:

- An auto-responder automatically sends e-mails without human involvement.

- Sends personalized messages at a specified time, or e-mails follow-ups automatically.

- Will work for you 24 hours a day, 7 days a week until you discontinue its use.

- **Sendfree.com** provides statistics on how your auto-responder is performing.

- **Freeautobot.com** sends out unlimited auto-response

messages that you have set up.

As mentioned in Chapter 9, building rapport with your clients by being considerate and asking for their input to your business is critical to customer satisfaction and the overall reputation of your business, as well as establishing yourself as a trustworthy businessperson. Always ask questions, listen, and give the impression of genuine understanding. Questions to ask potential clients visiting your Web site:

1. What type of home do you desire?

2. How many bedrooms and bathrooms are you looking for?

3. Have you considered the location or areas of town you would like me to search for you?

4. What things are a must for you and are not negotiable?

5. What is your loan approval amount, and what amount are you comfortable with?

Other tips for advertising through one-on-one contact include: selling your prospect on your other services by letting your other business endeavors be made known to your real-estate customer, contacting people you know in other business fields and asking about a referral contract, and asking for friendly referrals from the potential customer who may lead you to other buyers.

Chapter 10 teaches us how to buy advertising, and how to

use Google for pay-per-click advertising. Key points in this area are as follows:

- Figure out where your prospects are most likely to spend time online, and buy into advertising in those places.

- Shop aggressively for ads, review your results often, and adjust as needed.

- Use AdSense and AdWords, which are programs powered by Google, to bring a multitude of customers to your "doorstep" with pay-per-click advertising options.

- Yahoo offers "pay per performance," which allows you to test the waters to see the number of clicks on each of your sample ads before buying into one.

Here are some pay-per-click marketing tactics:

- Compare PPC pricing models and offerings to find the best deals.

- If you have a limited budget, use do-it-yourself PPC outlets.

- If your time available is limited, enlist the help of a search engine marketing expert.

- Maintain your PPC budget by using localized pay-per-click advertising.

Banner ads are essentially an image with embedded HTML

code that acts as a hyperlink when launched, as is explained in Chapter 11. The common way of charging for banner ads is by using a "pay-per-click" system.

Reasons a business may choose a banner ad:

- Drives more Web traffic to your Web site.

- Boosts sales of your products and services.

- Alerts your customers to any special deals you are offering or any new listings or services that you have.

- Publicizes your name on the Internet so potential clients know who you are.

- When a banner ad is displayed, the hyperlink attached to that ad directs the user to a certain Web page.

Chapter 12 focuses on affiliate marketing, and using these programs to generate leads through cash incentives. Three separate entities are involved in implementing affiliate programs. These are:

1. The Web site of the affiliate

2. Your business Web site

3. The Web visitor or customer who you are trying to attract to your Web site.

There are currently three methods used to pay affiliate participants:

1. Pay-per-click

2. Pay-per-lead

3. Pay-per-sale

You can become a part of an affiliate program by finding the affiliate networking site that best fits your needs, filling out the forms with your personal information and information about your Web site, and waiting for the application to be accepted by the administrator on the affiliate program's site. Affiliate ads link to your Web site through:

1. Banner ad links

2. Text and content links

3. Co-branding

Blogs can greatly enhance your image. Chapter 13 explains how to choose a blog domain name that is unique and relevant to the content. Other helpful hints also found in Chapter 13 include:

• Write only about a niche market

• Use search engine optimized keywords.

Free resource Web sites for blogging:

- Blogger

- Blogology

- Real Estate Blog Service

Exchanging links with other Web sites and with other bloggers gets your blog seen.

Keep the content fresh on your blog. To get more leads from people inquiring about your services as a result of your blog heed the following advice:

- Add new informative blog posts often

- Invite visitors to make comments

- Link to online virtual tours of your listings

- Always be positive

- Include a newsletter subscription on your blog page

Chapter 14 sheds light on using eBay as a means of advertising your property listings. Here are the basic steps to take to use this method of advertisement:

- Obtain a screen name that matches your main Web site name, and make sure your seller profile has good ratings. Choose one of the following types of listing:

1. Auction/Fixed-price format

2. Classified ad

Keep up with your inquiries, as there will be many if you choose to use eBay. Always give feedback when the transaction is complete. Keep a file of interested buyers to refer back to when you have properties that fit their needs.

Chapter 15 delineates the ins and outs of hiring help to advertise and keep yourself organized. Hiring for each project is important because you can get a much lower rate when using several freelancers to do small jobs, rather than one to do all the jobs you want to outsource. Here are some helpful hints to remember before hiring:

- Payment should be agreed upon beforehand.

- Decide on how often payments should be sent and in what form.

- Ask for a sample of writing style before hiring.

- Check all the free media for advertising such as Craigslist and Elance.

Hiring an individual who is organized and skilled to keep you on track is one way of shortening and consolidating your workload. Remember to do the following things before taking on a potential candidate as your virtual assistant:

- Interview applicants thoroughly.

- Find out their hours and work details.

- Review work history.

- Have applicants do a small test project to confirm skill level.

Resource Web sites:

- **www.craigslist.com**

- **www.rentacoder.com**

- **www.getafreelancer.com**

- **www.elance.com**

Remember that freelancers are always searching for work, and it is easy to find someone to complete your projects if you know where to look.

BIBLIOGRAPHY

A Touch of Business. (2007). *Learn Why Search Engine Optimization Is So Important.* Retrieved November 8, 2007, from **www.atouchofbusiness.com/business-topics/website-tips/Search-Engine-Optimization-0050.html.**

Achatz, W. & Pliska, R. J. (2001). *Using Technology to Enhance Your Real Estate Business.* Eau Claire, WI: National Business Institute.

AlignMark, Inc. (2007). *Recommendations for Improvement of Sales Skills and Abilities.* Retrieved on November 8, 2007, from **www.realestatesimulator.com/broker_resources/tips.htm.**

Answers Corporation. (2007). *E-mail Marketing.* Retrieved on November 8, 2007, from **www.answers.com/topic/e-mail-marketing?cat=biz-fin.**

Bannan, K. J. (2007). *A Few Tips for Making the Unsubscribe Process Better for All.* Retrieved on November 8, 2007, from **www.btobonline.com/apps/pbcs.dll/article?AID=/20070312/FREE/70312028/1109/FREE.**

Barrell, D. & Nash, M. W. (2005). *Fundamentals of Marketing for the Real Estate Professional.* Chicago, IL: Dearborn Real Estate Education.

Brown, B. C. (2006). *How to Use the Internet to Advertise, Promote, and Market Your Web Site with Little or No Money.* Ocala, FL: Atlantic Publishing Group.

Carolinanet.com. (2007). *E-mail Server Colocation.* Retrieved on November 8, 2007, from **www.carolinanet.com/email_colocation. php.**

Collins, G. (2007). *PPC Advertising – Pay-per-Click Programs.* Retrieved on November 8, 2007, from **www.seoconsultants.com/ articles/1383/pay-per-click-programs.asp.**

Cox, B. G. & Koelzer, W. (2001). *Internet Marketing in Real Estate.* Upper Saddle River, NJ: Prentice Hall.

Cox, B. G. & Koelzer, W. (2001). *Web Marketing for the Real Estate Professional.* Upper Saddle River, NJ: Prentice Hall.

Duermyer, R. (2007). *Pay Per Click Advertising (PPC).* Retrieved on November 8, 2007, from **homebusiness.about.com/od/ internetmarketing/a/pay_per_click.htm.**

ElectricNews.Net Ltd. (2007). *Keep Business Contacts Up-to-date.* Retrieved on November 8, 2007, from **www.dceb.ie/opencontent/ default.asp?itemId=169.**

Flick, F. E. (1999). *Real Estate and Technology: Realtors and the New Business Environment.* Chicago, IL: The Association.

Giesener, J. (2007). *Entries Categorized "Marketing – E-mail."* Retrieved on November 8, 2007, from **thegies.typepad.com/ runtosurvive/marketing_email/index.html.**

GoogAd.com (2006). *About Us.* Retrieved on November 8, 2007, from **www.googad.com/index.php/Default/About.html.**

Heng, C. (2007). *How to Make Autoresponders Work for You.* Retrieved on November 8, 2007, from **www.thesitewizard.com/ archive/autoresponders.shtml.**

Implix. (2007). *Big Benefits from Super-Powered Autoresponders.* Retrieved on November 8, 2007, from **www.getresponse.com/ articles/smart.html.**

INS Digital Media LLC. (2007). *PPC Advertising Tips.* Retrieved on November 8, 2007, from **www.squidinternet.com/internet-marketing/ppc_advertising_tips.htm.**

Janisch, K. (2006). "Technology Statistics." In *Field Guide to Quick Real Estate Statistics.* Retrieved November 8, 2007, from **www. realtor.org/libweb.nsf/pages/fg006#topice.**

Kimmons, J. (2007). *Top 5 Strategies for Writing an Effective Real Estate Pay-per-c.* Retrieved on November 8, 2007, from **realestate.about. com/od/realestatewebsites/tp/write_ppc_ad.htm.**

McDonald, L. (2004). *28 Ways to Build Permission-Based E-mail Lists.* Retrieved on November 8, 2007, from **www.emaillabs.com/ email_marketing_articles/building-email-list.html.**

McDonald, L. (2004). *Optimizing E-mail Opt-in Pages.* Retrieved on November 8, 2007, from **www.emaillabs.com/email_marketing_ articles/opt_in_pages.html.**

McDonald, L. (2005). *Permission E-mail Marketing: "Permission" Is Not Optional.* Retrieved on November 8, 2007, from **www. emaillabs.com/email_marketing_articles/permission_email_ marketing_matters.html.**

Nacht, R. & Chaney, P. (2007). *Realty Blogging: Build Your Brand and Outsmart Your Competition.* New York, NY: McGraw-Hill.

Pollard, S. (2007). *How to Grow Your Opt-in List: The Ultimate Guide.* Retrieved on November 8, 2007, from **www.emaillabs. com/email_marketing_articles/email_list_building.html.**

Richard, D. G. (2004). *Real Estate Rainmaker: Guide to Online Marketing.* Hoboken, NJ: John Wiley and Sons.

Robbins, C. (1999). *Real Estate Internet Skills One-Day Course.* New York, NY: DDC Publishing.

Search Engine Blog. (2006). *PPC Advertising – Pay-per-Click Programs.* Retrieved on November 8, 2007, from **www. esearchengineblog.com/ppc-advertising-pay-per-click-programs.asp.**

Search Engine Watch. (2007) *Worldwide Internet: Now Serving 61 Billion Searches per Month.* Retrieved on November 8, 2007, from **searchenginewatch.com/showPage.html?page=3627304.**

SEO and Marketing Resources. (2007). *SEO and Marketing Resources.* Retrieved on November 8, 2007, from **www.whitehatfirm.com/ seo-marketing-resources.**

Silverman, G. (1996). *How and Why to Research Word of Mouth.* Retrieved on November 8, 2007, from **www.quirks.com/articles/ a1996/19961209.aspx?searchID=3435187**.

Sofizar.net. (2007). *Performance Based Search Engine Optimization.* Retrieved on November 8, 2007, from **www.sofizar.net/pay-per-click-management.php.**

Swanepoel, S. (2000). *Real Estate Confronts the E-consumer*. Aliso Viejo, CA: RealSure, Inc.

Wikipedia.org. (2007). *E-mail Marketing*. Retrieved on November 8, 2007, from **en.wikipedia.org/wiki/Email_marketing.**

BIOGRAPHY

Karen F. Vieira, MSM, Ph.D.

Karen Vieira is a freelance Medical, Scientific and Technical Writer. She has published several scientific manuscripts in reputable journals such as Journal of Biological Chemistry and Nutrition Journal. Prior to becoming a writer, she worked full time as a health and wellness research scientist for Kraft Foods in the Nutrition Research department.

Vieira gained her Ph.D. in Molecular Biology from the College of Medicine at the University of Florida. She also received a B.S. in Molecular Biology from Florida Institute of Technology and a M.S. in Management from the MBA program at the University of Florida.

Karen is an entrepreneur and enjoys writing business plans, investing in real estate and being involved in start-up businesses. Her first real estate investment was in 2001 and since then she has been involved in real estate transactions and investments. She started her first Internet business in 2003 and has since used the Internet as a medium for marketing all her business ideas with the help of her husband, Christopher, an Internet marketing guru. Karen lives in West Palm Beach, Florida with her husband and daughter, where she reads, exercises and gardens as a hobby and also enjoys the beach, snorkeling, and other water sports.

INDEX

A

Advantage 11, 13, 15

Advertising 12-15, 29,
37, 38, 41, 43-45, 49,
53, 54, 57, 59, 61,
83, 93, 111, 121, 122,
141, 157, 158, 160,
164, 169, 175-182,
184-188, 190, 192-199,
203, 206, 207, 213,
215, 216, 218-220,
232, 257, 258, 260,
265-269, 272, 273

Affiliate 201, 202, 203,
204, 205, 206, 207,
208, 209, 210, 211,
212, 213, 214, 215, 216

Agent 15, 17, 18, 20, 96,
99, 102, 119, 120, 134,
139, 142, 143, 180,
204, 216-220, 229, 248

B

Banner 175-199, 269,
271

Blog 118, 217-232, 265,
271, 272

Broker 15, 20, 33, 35,
124, 139, 204, 216,
217, 219, 236, 248

Budget 172, 173, 243,
246, 253-255

Buyer 17, 19, 25, 26, 28,
36, 43, 45, 120, 121,
139, 151

C

Campaign 93, 100, 107, 111, 127, 168-171

Click-through 127, 128

Client 59, 60, 65, 72-75, 86, 102, 134, 150, 152-157, 161, 162, 167, 181, 182, 186, 195, 204, 217, 218, 221, 224, 232

Communication 157, 159

Competition 218

Consumer 50, 167

Contact 49, 51, 56-58

Content 52, 54, 55, 258, 261, 262, 264, 265, 271, 272

Contract 248

Credit 58, 107

Customer 37, 44

D

Design 93, 95-97, 103, 106, 113, 115

Directory 59-65, 79

Domain 37, 39, 60, 170, 171

E

eBay 15, 235-241

F

Feedback 237, 241, 253

I

Information 18, 19, 21-28, 93, 97, 102, 104, 106, 115, 116, 118, 120, 124

Internet 11, 12, 14, 15, 17, 18, 21, 24, 61, 64, 65, 68, 126, 129, 135, 138, 147, 148, 166, 170, 176-182, 185-191, 193, 194, 196, 198

K

Keyword 70-72, 74, 76, 77, 89, 97, 98, 100, 102, 104, 105, 108, 109, 114, 116, 262

L

Leads 240

Links 19, 21, 22, 23, 118, 119, 120, 121

List 149, 150, 156, 161, 162

Listing 103, 104

Loan 108

M

Marketing 11-15, 18, 21, 22, 25, 28, 31-34, 37, 38, 43, 45-47, 54, 57, 60, 64, 68, 70, 89-91, 93, 95, 101, 103, 105, 109-111, 116, 117, 119, 122, 124, 126-128, 134-136, 139, 143, 147, 157-160, 163-165, 169, 172, 177, 181, 188, 202, 205, 207, 210, 216-220, 223, 229, 230, 232, 236

Message 126, 135, 140-142

Mortgage 19, 20, 25, 28, 185

N

Navigation 121
Newsletter 130, 131, 143

O

Online 17, 18, 19, 20, 21, 22, 24, 28, 29, 31, 34, 37, 39, 41, 43

Optimization 15, 98, 99, 100, 101, 103, 105, 106

Opt-in 126, 128, 130, 131, 132

Opt-out 126-128, 135

P

Pay-Per-Click 14, 15, 22, 83, 110, 163, 164, 167, 168, 169, 170, 171, 172, 173, 257, 269, 270

Permission 125, 126, 127, 128, 131, 136

Promote 44

Property 18, 117, 118, 120, 178, 180, 182, 186-188, 191, 236-240

R

Rank 71, 83-86, 91

Ranking 96, 97, 100, 103, 109, 111, 113, 114

Real Estate 11-13, 15, 17-23, 25, 26, 48, 49-52, 54, 57, 58, 96-98, 99, 102, 105, 107, 108, 114, 120, 142, 150, 157, 159, 160, 175, 176, 178, 180, 183, 185, 186, 198, 203, 205-207, 210, 211, 215-221,

223, 225, 228, 230,
231, 232, 235, 236,
240, 241, 248, 249,
258, 260, 261, 266
Realtor 223, 224, 229,
231
Registration 126, 129,
131
Research 98, 109, 126
Resource 11, 23, 102,
108

S

Search Engine 15, 59-62,
69-84, 86-88, 91,
96-105, 108, 112, 113,
163, 169, 172, 221, 228
Service 156, 160
Software 71, 72, 74, 75,
76, 81
Spam 88
Strategy 21, 23, 25, 59,
60, 72, 83, 221, 229
Submission 61, 62, 63,
64

T

Tactics 14
Tags 98, 100, 102, 104,
105, 109, 111, 112, 116

Techniques 188, 202,
207, 223
Traffic 83, 85, 86, 87, 88

V

Virtual Tour 117, 265
Visibility 14

W

Web Design 117, 121,
123, 124
Web site 11, 12-15,
18-29, 31, 32, 34,
37-49, 51-55, 57,
59-66, 69-74, 76-79,
81-90, 117-126, 129,
131, 139, 144, 145,
164, 166, 168-170,
175, 176, 179-184,
186-188, 190, 191,
193, 195-199, 201-206,
208, 209, 211-216,
247, 249, 252, 254-256
Web Site 93, 100, 106,
114